Grahame Knox and Chris Chesterton

First published 1992

ISBN 0 86201 813 7

British Library Cataloguing-in-Data
A catalogue record for this book is available from the British Library.

Book and cover design by Tony Cantale Graphics
Additional artwork by James Walton, a pupil at Gedling Comprehensive School, Nottingham

Printed and bound in Great Britain by Ebenezer Baylis and Son Ltd, The Trinity Press, Worcester

ACKNOWLEDGEMENTS

The authors would like to thank Robin King, B P Owen, Allan Woolley and Dr Richard Montgomery for their ideas used in four of the assemblies.

The illustrations in **Another fine mess** are quoted from *The Book of Heroic Failures* by Stephen Pile (MacDonald Futura, 1979)

The story of Mr P Derksen in **Money, money, money** is quoted from *Consequences – Leaders Guide* by Emlyn Williams (Scripture Union, 1985)

The list of phobias in **Facing fear** are taken from *The Top Ten of Everything* by Russell Ash (Queen Ann Press, 1990)

The illustrations in **Facing the future** are taken from *Towards 2001: A Consumer Guide to the 21st Century* by Abrams and Bernstein (Angus and Robertson, 1990)

The assembly **Christmas unwrapped** was first published in the *Christmas Unwrapped Schools Pack* by Grahame Knox and Caroline Ray (Christmas Unwrapped, 1990)

A
REALLY
GREAT
ASSEMBLY

Contents

Introduction

This book, a sequel to *Assembly Point* by Grahame Knox and David Lawrence (Scripture Union, 1990), is designed to equip you – the Christian visitor to the school – with a range of assembly ideas so that you can take up the challenge of leading school worship, and to do so effectively and in a way acceptable to the school. The outlines in *Assembly Point* concentrated on explaining key aspects of Christian belief as they relate to our everyday lives. *A Really Great Assembly* provides Christian assemblies dealing with wider issues about the world, our place in it and issues which affect our lifestyle. It takes a look at our feelings and emotions and how they affect the way we live and also includes more assembly outlines for Christmas, Easter and Pentecost.

Start here

The 1988 *Education Reform Act,* with its requirements for a daily act of 'broadly Christian worship' for every pupil, has presented a real challenge. Many teachers feel unable to lead Christian worship, perhaps because they do not themselves share Christian beliefs or perhaps because they simply do not have the time to prepare adequately alongside their other commitments. In some schools Christian teachers and pupils top the list of those asked to lead worship in the school assembly; in other areas many heads and teachers have turned to local churches to help resource them as they seek to implement the worship provisions of the 1988 Act.

In this book we make the assumption that as a visitor to the school you will be invited in because you represent the Christian faith or a local Christian church. It is our experience that, on this basis, the teacher in charge will expect you to be fairly open in your explanation of the Christian faith and what it means to you to be a Christian.

Taking aim

It is important to realise that the school is not providing an opportunity to evangelise, that is, to call people to a personal commitment to Christ. It is hardly fair to preach to a captive audience and doing so will only alienate both young people and staff. There is no reason, however, why we should not present the Christian gospel in an assembly. We do not need to apologise for our faith. We do, however, need to be sensitive in our presentation. For example, because the majority of participants in school worship are unlikely to share our commitment to

Christianity, we should not ask them to say or do things that assume a commitment.

We must also avoid presenting Christian truth in such a way that pupils are 'cornered'. That is, if they don't make the right response – the one you ask for – the only other option you leave for them is to accept that they are wrong. We should be cautious about any hint of indoctrination in what we say or the way we say it. Avoid making dogmatic statements or giving the pupils the impression that you are telling them what to believe. Instead, share from your own experience using phrases like, 'I believe that...' or 'Christians believe that...'. In this way we can still challenge the assumptions of our hearers and stimulate them to think about the issue raised in the assembly. Remember that your assembly can give young people a positive picture of those who have faith in God and a positive picture of God himself.

The Act and all that...

The 1988 Act requires that all pupils must be involved in a 'collective act of worship' every school day, which is 'wholly or mainly of a broadly Christian character.' Some explanations might be helpful here.

Assembly and worship

Under the 1988 Act 'assembly' and 'worship' are differentiated. An assembly is the time when the whole school or parts of the school, such as year groups, are gathered together for notices and other administrative purposes and perhaps to foster the school's ethos. All staff and pupils are obliged to be present. The act of worship is distinct from this and both staff and pupils have the right to opt out of it. Assemblies do not have to take place every day, but every pupil is supposed to be involved in a school act of worship every day, unless withdrawn by his or her parents or guardians.

Generally, the two activities of assembly and worship are put together in a single slot. In this book we assume you will be invited into such a situation and so refer to the entire slot as an 'assembly'. The time you are allocated within it may also vary from school to school but it will rarely be more than ten minutes.

Collective worship

Collective worship should be distinguished from corporate worship. By using the term 'collective', the Act acknowledges that although staff and pupils have gathered together to participate in or observe an act of Christian worship, they do not necessarily share the Christian faith. At the same time, the Act seems to assume that a group of people from different faiths or of no faith at all can participate in an activity which to some degree reflects Christian worship. Not all Christians share this view. In contrast to collective worship, the worship of a body of committed Christians would be described as 'corporate'.

'... wholly or mainly of a broadly Christian character'

Beliefs and practices presented in school

worship are of a 'broadly Christian character' if they are accepted across a broad spectrum of mainstream Christian denominations. It would be unacceptable to speak of practices unique to a particular denomination as though they were the practice of all Christians. The material included in an act of worship need not be drawn 'wholly' from Christian sources. Indeed, it can be far more effective to explain a Christian truth by using material from writers, artists, politicians etc who might not claim to have any religious beliefs.

Assembly outlines

In every assembly outline you will find:

An introduction This explains the aim of the assembly and what you will need to do in the way of preparation before the event.

Content This explains how to introduce the assembly and outlines the main parts of the assembly input. As you use the material in this section you should aim to 'personalise' it where possible by adding your own anecdotes and any topical stories in the news or popular TV programmes. Prepare well enough beforehand so that you do not have to use the book in an assembly; a story told is much more gripping than a story read.

Application and response The 1988 Act specifies that 'worship' should happen in schools on a formal basis. We believe that in a context where probably the majority of pupils are unlikely to be practising Christians, it is fair to interpret 'worship' in terms of 'response'. The 'application and response' section in the assembly outline draws out the point of the content and suggests an appropriate response to the assembly content.

The type of response can vary enormously. It could be simply an increased awareness or understanding of an aspect of Christian truth, perhaps as a result of learning from the experience of others. It could be a sense of awe and wonder, evoked by what has been shared from the platform. It could be a change in attitude, such as the development of respect for something previously dismissed without thought. It could be a moment's reflection on the meaning and purpose of life. Or it could be the desire to take some practical action in response to a challenge to do so, such as organising an event to raise money for charity.

It may sometimes be appropriate to include prayer as a response. A prayer of thanks or praise could be read out for the pupils to listen to and, if they wish, make their own. This will, of course, depend on the sort of material that has been presented and on the usual practice of the school. Make a point of asking the head teacher, or whoever takes responsibility for the assemblies, whether it would be acceptable to include a prayer. If you do decide to include a prayer it is important to introduce it with a phrase that allows the young people to opt out of saying it. You could say, for instance, 'I am going to say/read a short prayer now. As I do, think about the words. You might like to close your eyes to help you concentrate. If you agree with what the prayer says and want to make it your own, say "Amen" at the end, which simply means "I agree".' Make your closing prayer short and to the point.

An alternative to saying or reading a prayer is simply to leave a few seconds of silence after you have presented your material. Suggest that pupils use it to think over what they have heard, perhaps thinking about one point they found particularly helpful, interesting or outrageous – or to pray silently.

And finally...

The assembly outlines in this book are all designed for secondary schools. We have not included details about the age range they can be used with. This is because we believe that you, the reader, are best placed to find out about your audience and to determine the maturity and background of the pupils. We are also aware that most assembly takers adapt, add or remove material from the outlines to fit the age group and time available. Many assemblies, adjusted in this way, can be used across a wide age range.

Not all the material in this book will suit every assembly leader or be appropriate for use in every school. Be selective, adapt and develop the ideas given in this book in order to make them more 'you'. Most of the assemblies in this book are designed for one person (sometimes with 'volunteers' from the audience) and only require minimal props. Our hope is that this book will encourage you to take many thought-provoking assemblies and will inspire you to create lots more of your own. The remaining part of this first section gives some thoughts on how to move beyond this book and develop your own assembly ideas.

Finding themes and ideas

We lead busy lives and all too often the time available for preparing a school assembly is limited. The trouble is, good talks often take a long time to develop. A 'seed' idea may 'germinate' in the subconscious and only 'flower' weeks, months, or even years later. In order to sow lots of these 'seeds' for a future harvest, why not start a file or folder? It could contain page references to things you have noted in books, notes on stories and testimonies you have heard, newspaper cuttings, facts and figures, illustrations that might be copied onto OHP/ transparencies, songs and prayers, etc. If you are not that organised, even a collection of back-of-envelope jottings can be very helpful! Here are some places to look for those 'seeds'.

The Bible

The Bible is our chief source book. Why not keep a slip of paper in your Bible to jot down any ideas that occur to you during your regular Bible reading? Try reading one of the Gospels to see which stories and teaching are particularly relevant to your target age-group. See these stories with fresh eyes by 'translating' them into today's world. For instance, the paralysed man was brought to Jesus on a mat (Luke 5). Today's equivalent might be a wheelchair. This might suggest a suitable visual aid or other way into the story.

The natural world

'For since the creation of the world God's invisible qualities – his eternal power and divine nature – have been clearly seen, being understood from what has been made, so that men are without an excuse' (Romans 1:20). 'Look at the birds of the air ... See how the lilies of the field grow ...' (Matthew 6:26 and 28). 'The heavens declare the glory of God; the skies proclaim the work of his hands ...' (Psalm 19:1).

God has provided us with an almost infinite book of illustrations and parables – the universe he has created! Plants, animals, the stars, scientific research – all are displaying 'God's invisible qualities'. We can help young people to discover truth and a sense of wonder and to 'see the invisible' for themselves in nature.

Books, books, books

Look over your own bookshelves. Biographies (Christian or not), humorous anecdotes, nature or science books, travel books, etc, etc. Most of us, especially if we have children, have a host of untapped material already sitting waiting at home.

In **A most amazing machine** (page 30), for example, a few facts out of a book have been turned into a stimulating assembly. Newspapers and magazines provide a virtually endless supply of human interest stories that can be used to good effect as illustrations.

Questions young people ask

Who made God? Why does God allow suffering? Hasn't science disproved the Bible? What happens when we die? This last question forms the basis of **Death – the Beginning?** (page 50). A clear, simple approach to one of these questions, especially with a telling illustration, is an ideal topic. Think how the relevant information might be presented dramatically or visually.

Common misconceptions

This overlaps with the 'Questions' approach. Things like: Jesus never really existed; Christianity is just a crutch for people who can't stand on their own feet; You can't trust the Bible because it was written long after the events; All roads lead to God. It needs a strong illustration or an incontrovertible fact powerfully presented to make people think again.

Your experience

Our own experience of Christ is a powerful witness that what we are saying really changes peoples' lives. We are living proof that it works! We are part of the message we present, a living visual aid for the work of Christ in our lives. Never underestimate the power of retelling your own experience, the ups and the downs, as a real life example of the Holy Spirit effecting change.

God's visual aids

Words are our prime means of communication, but words alone may have little lasting impact. Experience and research show that nine-tenths of what we hear is immediately forgotten. How much of the latest news broadcast you heard do you remember now? It can be frustrating to spend time and effort in preparing an assembly only to realise from the glazed looks in pupils' eyes that very little is going in. So how can we improve on that one-tenth?

The master communicator is God himself. Let's consider the range and variety of visual and dramatic teaching aids that God uses, and learn from him. Here are some of the many found in the Bible to stimulate your own thinking:

• **The rainbow.** No modern laser display can match God's glorious arc of light in the sky. What a reminder of his promise through Noah to mankind! (See Genesis 9:8–17.) What can we learn from this? It encourages us to use colour; to be big and bold; to leave symbols where they can be seen as a reminder. Many secondary schools can be drab places compared to their primary feeder schools. For example, to accompany **The parable of the three Cokes** (page 70) large 'smiles' and 'frowns' could be cut out of red craft paper. Displayed on the wall, they would arouse interest as soon as the pupils came in to the assembly and could act as a reminder afterwards.

• **The burning bush** (Exodus 3:1–4). This is not a symbol but an attention-grabber. Moses cannot ignore 'this strange sight'; his curiosity is awakened and he has to find out what is going on. Another example is the writing on the wall in Daniel 5. We can use 'strange sights' to make the pupils sit up and take notice. An example is the activities at the beginning of **Waist-high waste** (page 64). As we give them the answer, we slip the teaching point through the door opened by their curiosity.

• **The siege of Jerusalem dramatised** (Ezekiel 4). This is less familiar than the previous two examples, but just one of several instances where God is the script-writer and Ezekiel the one-man drama. The prophet enacts the prophecy before he pronounces it. Again, this has the effect of stimulating curiosity, so that when the spoken word comes it falls on ready ears. The more unusual and bizarre the drama – and some of God's scripts for Ezekiel are certainly that! – the greater the impact on the audience.

• **A ruined belt** (Jeremiah 13:1–11). As Ezekiel is the master of the dramatised lesson, so Jeremiah makes good use of the object lesson. In this instance, God tells the prophet to buy a new linen belt, bury it, then retrieve it later when it has been spoilt. Jeremiah can then show it to the people: it has become an object lesson of the uselessness of the people. Other examples are the two baskets of figs in Jeremiah 24 and the useless vine in Ezekiel 15. In each case an everyday object becomes a metaphor for a message from God. It then becomes a regular reminder of that message as people see it in their daily life.

• **A catch of fish and a charcoal fire** (John 21:1–14). In his resurrection appearance by the Sea of Galilee, Jesus gives his disciples two gentle but pointed reminders of the past. The netful of fish after a fruitless night's work recalls the the day that Jesus first called them to follow him (Luke 5:1–11). Then, as Peter gazes at the charcoal fire on the beach, he cannot help but remember his denial of Jesus by the similar fire in the high priest's courtyard. (John 18:18 and 21:9 are the only places in the New Testament where this word for a fire is used.) This is a wonderful example of Jesus' powerful but indirect way of making people think. It should help us to be wary of the sledge-hammer approach of spelling everything out.

• **A granddaddy of a storm** (Job 38:1–3). Job quails before the power of the storm and realises his insignificance. Many young people picture God as a sort of benign uncle: nice if you need him, but easily ignored if you do not. If 'the fear of the Lord is the beginning of knowledge' (Proverbs 1:7), then we may serve young people well by helping them to see the power of the Creator behind the forces of nature.

From good idea to great assembly

So you have a story or idea that you feel would be good for Year 9 on Thursday morning. How do you turn that into an effective assembly? This outline may help you.

1 Formulate

What is the ONE thought, question, challenge, impression or image you want the pupils to retain? Formulate this aim and express it in one simple sentence. If you are not clear about your aim, the pupils may take away a confused message.

2 Factors

Review the important factors. What is the age-range, maturity and background of the pupils? How much time will you actually have after notices, presentations, etc? What resources do you have in terms of helpers, OHPs, music or materials?

3 Focus

How will you get the pupils to focus their attention on your message? Will it be through visual aids, drama, music, testimony, a story, involving pupils as volunteers, or some other method?

4 Framework

Once you have the main elements of your presentation, they should be built into a clear framework. You need:

- An introduction. Decide what your first sentence will be. It might be a question, a controversial statement, or asking for a volunteer. Make it crisp and confident.
- A clear development. This is the main part of your presentation. Make sure that different elements flow into one another smoothly. Will the pupils understand what is happening? Will interest be maintained?
- A conclusion. This might be one clearly stated sentence that offers a challenge, or a question to ponder on. Decide how to move from this into prayer, silent reflection, singing or listening to a song, or however else the assembly is to conclude.

You may wish to transfer this framework in the form of headings onto a piece of card or paper to refer to during the assembly.

5 Forethought

Avoid last-minute panics by a little forethought. Make a check-list of props or visual aids needed. If other people are involved, make sure they know when and where to be. If you are a visitor travelling to a school, plan a departure time from home that takes rush-hour traffic into account. Have the school telephone number to hand in case of emergencies.

6 Fear not!

Speaking to a large number of young peop1e can be nerve-racking. Confidence comes from knowing your material well. If you are using visual aids or doing some kind of demonstration, practice beforehand. Find out what can go wrong at home rather than at school! Stories and drama should be thoroughly rehearsed. Weed out any jargon or words likely not to be understood by the pupils. Cut out any needless repetition. Remember your prime aim and eliminate additional messages that have crept in. Check timing (and find out from experience whether you normally run longer or shorter than your rehearsal when you do the real thing).

If you have measured your material against this outline, you can go out in the confidence that your assembly will present a clear message and hold the attention of that hall full of young people.

Assembly hints

1 Making contact

If you are approaching the school yourself, decide on your initial point of contact with the school - a Christian teacher known to you, the head teacher or the member of staff responsible for the assembly. Be prepared for a healthy suspicion on the part of the school; a responsible school will not let just anybody in to take an assembly. Be prepared to outline the material you may be using. If possible, make your offer to a school where you already have links with staff or pupils.

2 Be prepared!

Offer to take assembly at a time when it will be of most help to the school: Christmas, Easter or Harvest; for example, not the first week of term or during exams. Find out when the assembly begins and ends and how much time will be allocated to you; what else will happen during the total assembly time (notices, sports results etc); what the normal pattern for assembly is and whether the school is happy to deviate from it. (For instance, is there always/sometimes/never a hymn or prayer?) Find out the age range of the pupils in the assembly and whether they comprise the whole school or simply part of it; whether pupils from other faiths will be present and whether they will stay in for your talk. If so,which faiths do they represent, and if there is anything you should know about relationships between the faith groups in the school.

These questions will enable you to prepare your material and, in the eyes of the staff, will help to confirm your credibility.

3 Maintain goodwill

Don't turn up late. Arriving late piles on the stress for the staff as, at the last minute, they try to organise something else for the assembly. Aim to arrive at least twenty minutes before the assembly is due to begin. If it is your first visit, chatting to staff will help break down any barriers of uncertainty they may have about you. The way you respond to them is an important part of your witness. Don't go over time. The effect of what you have said will be completely lost if the bell goes before you have finished. You will lose the goodwill of the staff as they see their teaching day start late and with a chaotic rush to get to the first lesson.

4 Making assumptions?

Assume little or no previous knowledge of the Christian faith. Start from where the pupils are and move them on from the familiar to the unfamiliar. Avoid Christian clichés and jargon. Explain clearly what any unfamiliar words mean. Be prepared to address a wide range of issues. Talk about life, the universe and everything and look for 'signposts' to the gospel. Don't be afraid to raise questions as well as providing answers. Much of the value of poetry, drama and stories lie in their ability to open up the right questions rather than to offer specific answers.

5 Using humour

Use humour to open a way for your message. You do not have to be funny all the time, but being funny at least some of the time will help. Take great care, however, not to 'diminish' people by humour. Comedy and satire form a major part of the teenage TV diet, but an assembly that makes fun of other people inevitably carries an unspoken message about the way Christians regard and value others. Avoid making humorous comments about staff or school meals as this can easily backfire and cause offence.

6 Using volunteers

Involve pupils in the assembly. Many of the outlines in this book suggest that you do this: seeing friends up on the stage is part of what makes an assembly memorable for the rest of the school! However, you need to exercise care. Where the outlines suggest that you invite pupils to take part you can do so by one of these means:

- If you are confident that you can handle the unexpected, simply ask for volunteers on the spot.
- In advance, ask a teacher to give you names of pupils who they think would be happy to take part. You can then ask for these at the appropriate time.
- Arrange with pupils in advance so that they are fully briefed and prepared to take part with you. Remember to treat pupils with respect and never embarrass or belittle them on stage.

7 Working together

In many schools God has placed Christians to be 'salt and light' in their surroundings. They may be pupils, teachers, caretakers or secretaries, but once you leave the assembly hall it will be their ongoing Christian witness that will help your message to take root in people's minds.

When the initial contact is being made with the school try to find out whether there are any Christian staff at the school and if there is a CU or any other Christian group functioning in the school. Try to let them know about your planned assembly visit. Their comments and possible involvement will be helpful. If possible, meet to pray together before the assembly. Remember that your assembly will have a big impact on the credibility of Christians already in the school. You might build into the assembly some ideas and thought-starters that can be taken up by Christians in the school later in the day in their conversations with friends.

8 Using the Bible

• The Bible is God's living word. Reading it in a monotone is tantamount to manslaughter! Check out different versions to find which gives the clearest rendering of your chosen passage.

• Vary the length of passages. Often a sentence or two will crystallise the day's thought. On the other hand, a whole story well read can be a complete and challenging assembly in itself. Try a dramatic reading of the story of the healing of the blind man (John 9).

• A dramatised reading can be effective. *The Dramatised Bible* (Marshall Pickering / Bible Society) does all the preparation for you.

• Beware of using Bible verses out of context or to back up low-grade moralising. The teacher who was reading from Ecclesiastes, 'a time to be silent and a time to speak,' and who broke off to shout, 'And now is the time for you to be silent, lad!' is merely an extreme example of a not uncommon fault. Large numbers of an older generation lumped the Bible with school rules and were glad to put both behind them. Don't let us give the current generation of pupils the same excuse.

ASSEMBLY OUTLINES

OUR PLACE IN THE WORLD

1 Space – the final frontier

Introduction

- **Aim:** To encourage a sense of awe at the universe and at the Creator who planned and made it all.
- **Preparation:** You will need the biggest beach ball you can find (or football), a seed, two small marbles, a tennis ball and a pin.

Content

Explain that the morning's assembly is going to have an astronomical theme to it. Ask the pupils, 'Have you ever looked up at the stars at night and tried to count them, or tried to see the different constellations, or ever wondered how far away they were, or what they were like? The universe we live in is a huge and an amazing place.' (Use the facts given below to develop a sense of wonder at the vastness of space. Seek to create a sense of anticipation as you lead into the application and response section of the assembly.)

Planet Earth is the third planet in a solar system on the edge of the galaxy known as the Milky Way. Go on to explain that you are going to recreate the Solar System in miniature (well... part of it!) in the assembly hall. Ask for five volunteers to help you. Explain that if the Sun was a huge beach ball (or football) at the front of the hall, the nearest planet (Mercury) would be a small seed 50 feet away (about 16 paces).

Get one volunteer to hold up the beach ball on stage, the next volunteer to hold up the seed 50 feet away etc. Venus would be a marble about 95 feet away (31 paces) from the Sun; the Earth, a marble 130 feet away (45 paces); Mars, a pea 200 feet away (60 paces); Jupiter, a tennis ball 675 feet away from the Sun (225 paces).

By this time you should have run out of hall! If you have, ask the Jupiter volunteer to stand at the back of the hall holding the tennis ball in the air. Comment that the outermost planet, Pluto, would be a tiny pinhead about a mile away from our sun at the front of the hall. The nearest star would be thousands of miles away (somewhere in Africa). Our solar system is a pretty big place. (Thank the volunteers for their help.)

Go on to say that if it were possible to travel in a spacecraft at the speed of light you could go around the earth seven times in a second but to travel to the farthest galaxy that can be seen by the naked eye (the spiral galaxy of Andromeda) it would take about two million years travelling at the speed of light. In fact the farthest object discovered in the universe (a quasar in the constellation Ursa Major) is believed to be 14 billion light years away from Earth. The universe is a very big place!

The Solar System isn't just big but it's pretty amazing as well. For example the temperature deep inside the Sun is estimated to be 15 million degrees. If a pinhead (hold up pin) was that hot it would set light and destroy everything for miles around it. But did you know that Earth is EXACTLY the right distance from the Sun to support human life?

Application and response

'Faced with all this amazing information people have asked: Where did it all come from? We live in an amazing universe full of natural wonders and governed by laws obeyed by every galaxy, star, planet and moon. In fact science started because people believed they could see an order, a plan in the sky above them. Christians believe that order and plan was specially made, by someone bigger than even the universe itself, a being that even made time and space – GOD! They believe that his work can be seen in the order and beauty of the universe and it is totally dependent on him for its existence. That belief on its own is pretty mind-boggling, but it gets even more amazing. Christianity is founded on the belief that from beyond the vastness of the universe God made himself tiny enough to visit a very special planet, the Earth. He was born a baby, he grew up, talked with people and even claimed that it's possible for people like you and me to get to know God for ourselves ... (Pause)

'Well that's all we've got time for this morning! ... But let me leave you with a couple of thoughts. If there really is a God, and we are talking about a REALLY BIG God, how could you find out more about him? And if he visited the Earth, as millions of Christians throughout the world believe, what was his reason for coming?'

2 Spaceship Earth

Introduction

● **Aim:** To show that we have a responsibility for the world we live in and for others around us.

Content

Explain that you are going to start the assembly with a short quiz about the world we live in. Ask for a show of hands from the pupils after each question indicating whether they believe the statement to be true or false.

The first two questions concern people and are about hunger and water:

1. **More people have died as a consequence of hunger in the past five years than have been killed in all the wars, revolutions and murders in the past 150 years.** (TRUE)
2. **Half of the people who live in rural areas of the third world are without clean water.** (FALSE) Explain that in fact 7 out of 10 people don't have clean water. Did you know that more than three-quarters of all disease in the world is caused by polluted water?

The next two questions are about our environment. The first one is about acid rain. This is caused when air pollution from burnt fossil fuels mixes with water in the atmosphere. When the acid rain falls it destroys trees and pollutes rivers and lakes.

3. **In Norway four out of five rivers and lakes are too acidic for fish to survive.** (TRUE)
4. **Every minute an average of 50 acres of rainforest is cut down (equivalent to 30 football pitches)** (FALSE) In fact its double that figure; 60 football pitches every minute. Each year an area the size of Great Britain is cleared and about half of the world's tropical rainforests have already been destroyed.

Application and response

'The Earth is like a giant space capsule floating through space. It contains limited supplies of air, water and fuel. Mankind (and that includes you and me) has to take care to see the careful balance of nature is maintained or food supplies will be threatened and pollution could kill. Today many people are concerned about these important issues and believe they have a responsibility to try to change things and make the earth a better place to live in.

'Christians believe that they have a responsibility too, and not just to other

people, but a responsibility to God for the way they treat his creation, the Earth. A famous songwriter in the Bible, talking about our special responsibility, summed it up like this;

> You (God) appointed him (Man – ie
> people) ruler over everything
> you made;
> you placed him over all creation:
> sheep and cattle, and all the wild
> animals too;
> the birds and the fish
> and the creatures in the seas

'You will probably hear people give all sorts of different reasons for why we have human misery and environmental problems, but Christians believe the real cause actually lies deep in our hearts – the Earth is being spoiled and exploited because of greed and selfishness, people thinking only of their own comfort or seeing how much money they can make at the expense of others. Until there is a change of attitude in people's hearts the problems will continue.

'Everyone can play a part, however small, in stopping Spaceship Earth from being spoilt.' (You may wish to mention a local environmental campaign to illustrate this point.) 'But if, as Christians believe, it is really being spoilt because of our greed and selfishness, perhaps more important than a change of attitude is to have a "change of heart"?'

3 How big you are!

Introduction

- **Aim:** To give pupils a sense of their importance in the scheme of things.
- **Preparation:** You will need a ruler and a marked distance of twenty metres in the assembly hall.

Content

Ask for a volunteer who is suffering from a cold. Failing that, get someone out and ask them to imagine they have a cold. Get the volunteer to put his hand in front of his mouth and cough. Why do we protect our mouths with a hand or handkerchief when we cough? To catch the microbes and try to stop the infection spreading.

Ask the volunteer to hold out his hand. Can he see a cold virus on it? No; not surprising when you could get around ten thousand of them end to end in one millimetre!

Hold out a ruler and ask the volunteer to move his hand ten centimetres along it. Moving the tiny virus that far is the equivalent of a giant hand reaching down, picking one of us up, and carrying us two thousand kilometres!

Get your volunteer to carry the virus on a slightly longer journey: twenty metres to a marked point. That is like a giant hand carrying us right around the Earth more than ten times!

Now imagine the volunteer getting in a car and taking a quick 100 km trip down the motorway, still carrying his pet virus. It would only take an hour. That would be the same as the giant hand putting us aboard a spacecraft and taking us on a trip well beyond the orbit of the planet Saturn – one and a quarter billion miles, in fact!

Application and response

'Sometimes we look up at the stars and think how small we are. Often we add the word "insignificant" as well. But if we turn round and look the other way, through a microscope rather than a telescope, we realize just how big we are. Vast! Enormous!

'Size is a very poor way of measuring how significant things are. That virus could infect a President or a Prime Minister who could then have an off-day and make a bad decision that would affect the lives of millions of people.

'The Bible uses a quite different way of measuring us. It says we are made "in the image of God". There are things about us which are like the Creator himself. In our art and music and design we too are creative. We know right from wrong and can choose between them. Although we are not gods ourselves and never will be, Christians believe God's purpose for us is to join him in a life beyond death and beyond this universe. That makes us pretty significant.

'When we measure ourselves like that, size does not have too much to do with it. How big do you think you are now?'

4 A most amazing machine

Introduction

- **Aim:** To communicate a sense of wonder about the bodies God has given us.
- **Preparation:** You will need a lamb's kidney (a few pence from the butcher's) and a box to hold it in. (A shoe-box sprayed with metallic car-paint gives a good effect.)

Content

Announce that you have in the box one of the most amazing machines in the known universe. It performs a vital environmental task. Human and higher animal life would be impossible without it. This machine receives capsules containing a mixture of many different chemicals, some of them harmful. It unloads each capsule, sorts through the chemicals, removes thirty different harmful substances, and reloads the rest – 99% of the volume – back onto the capsule. To perform that immensely complex task it takes *just one secon*d. And it treats *billions* of capsules every hour. Ask the pupils if they would like to see this marvellous machine?

Hold up the kidney – and wait for the gasps of disgust! This is the machine, a kidney. We each have two of them in the small of our back. The capsules are red blood cells. Feel your pulse ... (demonstrate). Every heartbeat one-quarter of the blood is directed to the kidneys. In every heartbeat millions of red blood cells are being emptied; sugars, salts and water are handled separately, waste-products are removed to be flushed away in urine, and all the valuable chemicals are reloaded into the cells.

Some people's kidneys fail. If they are lucky, they are treated by dialysis machines. These machines cost thousands of pounds each. They are far larger than a human kidney and perform much less efficiently. Most of us are fortunate to have two that perform without a hitch for our seventy plus years. According to the experts, they are the second most amazing machines in the known universe. (The first is the human brain.)

Application and response

King David, the famous singer-songwriter in the Bible, lived too long ago to know the scientific details. But he was still struck by the wonder of the human body and praised God that he was wonderfully made. Close with his words from Psalm 139:13–16a;

> You created every part of me;
> you put me together in my mother's womb.
> I praise you because you are to be feared;
> all you do is strange and wonderful.
> I know it with all my heart.
> When my bones were being formed,
> carefully put together in my mother's womb,
> when I was growing there in secret,
> you knew I was there –
> you saw me before I was born.

5 Brain power

Introduction

- **Aim:** To enhance the pupils' sense of self-worth by showing how remarkable the human brain is.
- **Preparation:** Rehearse the computer game scenario or pre-record onto cassette to be played over a PA system.

Content

Read the following without any introduction. It should be read fast and urgently until the last sentence. This begins slowly and portenteously until the revelation of what it is all about.

'Red alert!! Cyborg mutants from Betelgeuse 2 are attacking Earth! Crouched over the forward view-screen of your hyper-space Earth-defence fighter ship, nerves screwed to a screaming-pitch of concentration, you know that you will have only six-tenths of one second from sighting the enemy to hitting the photon-torpedo fire-button. Failure to react in time will not only mean that you will be reduced to a cloud of incandescent plasma, but that the whole of Earth civilisation will be wiped out. Nothing but the

speed of your highly trained reactions stands between planet Earth and total annihilation! But if you succeed, you will earn not only the gratitude of the whole world ... but you will be rewarded with 5000 points and the chance to play again on level 4.'

Continue with something along these lines:

'Many of us enjoy video-games, whether at the arcade, on a home computer or a hand-held game. The computer hardware and software that makes them happen seems pretty clever. But compared to our brains, they are actually very primitive.

'Consider what is happening as we play that game. 127 million light-sensitive cells in our eyes are recording the swiftly changing patterns on the screen. 25,000 receptor cells in our ears are picking up the sound output. Other cells all over our bodies are transmitting details of the position of our fingers poised over the fire-button, and whether it is time to break off for a snack or a visit to the loo. Our brain is receiving 100 million messages every second. And that vast input of information occupies only one-tenth of one per cent of our brain cells. Two-tenths of one per cent more are controlling all our movement, from the finger on the button to the balancing act on the chair when we get too excited. In order to deal with all this massive input and output, those brain cells need to communicate with each other. They do that electrochemically. Every second within your brain there are five trillion chemical operations.'

Application and response

'Do you feel good about yourself? You should do. Carried around in that bony box on the top of your neck is the most highly advanced piece of equipment anywhere in the known universe. Next time you play a computer game, just think to yourself, "This may be smart, but God gave me a brain that's a million times smarter."'

6 Just another number

Introduction

- **Aim:** To encourage pupils to think that although we live in a world which can treat us impersonally, Christians believe that God treats us as special and unique individuals.
- **Preparation:** You will need to prepare the Magic Square grid on an OHP acetate and learn how to perform the illustration confidently and without reference to the book. You also need a calculator.

	1		7
	8		2
5		3	
4		6	9

a

Content

Start by explaining that the morning assembly is about numbers. Say that you are are going to perform an amazingly complex mathematical problem without the use of calculators or computers or a safety net! Reveal the grid for the Magic Square (a large square divided into 16 smaller squares). Explain that you are going to ask a pupil for a number between 50 and 100 and that you will place numbers in the square so that each row of numbers adds up to the pupil's number – vertically, diagonally and horizontally. Also the four corner numbers and the four centre squares will add up to the chosen number. (You may wish to have a volunteer with a calculator to confirm your claims about the square.)

1. Ask for a number between 50 and 100. Write the numbers one to nine in the squares shown in (a). You will see that with the first eight numbers each set of numbers going down vertically add up to nine. Then add the nine in the bottom right-hand square.
2. You then add the numbers 10, 11 and 12 in the positions shown in (b). You put the numbers one to twelve in these positions every time you present the Magic Square, regardless of the pupil's number. You are now left with four spaces to fill.
3. Subtract 21 from the pupil's chosen number – for example, if the number is 70, subtract 21 giving 49. Use the number you arrive at (49 in this example) and add the three numbers after it – 50, 51 and 52. Put

49 in the 'A' square, 50 in the 'B' square, 51 in the 'C' square and 52 in the 'D' square. You now have the Magic Square (c).

Ask the pupils (especially your volunteer with the calculator) to confirm that the number 70 is produced when four numbers are added up vertically, diagonally, horizontally, the four corners, the four centre squares.

Application and response

Explain that numbers are very important. We use numbers to tell the time, how old we are, we use numbers in history (1066 and all that), we use numbers in science, numbers tell us the speed things travel, they tell us when to get up, when school finishes each day.

Numbers can also be used to categorise us. People have a driving licence number, a national insurance number to pay tax, a bank account number, a national health number, an electoral roll (voting) number and you could probably think of other examples.

Continue with something along these lines:

'Numbers are important but they don't really tell other people what we are like; if we are kind or not, the things which concern us, the things which make us different. Sometimes people complain that they are "just another number" in some big computer and no one really cares about them as a real person. It's tempting, too, to think that if there really is a God who is looking after millions and millions of people on Earth we cannot really be very important. We are probably just another insignificant number.

'Christians are people that have learned that God's not like that. Amazingly he thinks that each one of us is very special, he made us and he knows all about us and takes an interest in everything we are doing. Just listen to what someone in the Bible said about that. This person knew he was special, and God says to us in the Bible that we are special as well.' Read Psalm 139:1–6.

B	1	12	7
11	8	A	2
5	10	3	D
4	C	6	9

b

50	1	12	7
11	8	49	2
5	10	3	52
4	51	6	9

c

7 Invisible danger

Introduction

- **Aim:** To help pupils evaluate religious ideas and philosophies.
- **Preparation:** You will need a freshly-made sandwich containing mayonnaise as part of the filling, and a brown paper bag.

Content

Ask who is hungry and would like a (whatever) and mayonnaise sandwich. Get a volunteer to come out and eat the sandwich. Ask if it tastes good. When they have finished, ask what they would think if you said it was home-made mayonnaise, made with fresh eggs, and it had been standing in a warm kitchen for several days? If necessary, remind them of salmonella and the dangers of food-poisoning. Send them back to their seat, but as they go say, 'By the way, take this brown paper bag. You may need it!'

Ask the pupils to put their hands up if they have ever been sick after eating 'something that disagreed with them'. Most will. Briefly mention any recent incidents reported in the press. A hamburger or a piece of chicken may look appetising but may contain invisible danger.

Application and response

Explain that the same is true of the ideas and beliefs that people put forward as being the answer to our personal problems or those of the world. 'How can we distinguish between what is really good and what may look good but actually be harmful? There is no quick or easy answer, but this is the advice Jesus gave:' (Read or have read Matthew 7:15–20.)

Continue with something along these lines:

'Jesus is saying, run some tests; don't judge by first impressions or the claims people make; see what actually happens in practice.

'Earlier this century many people were taken in by the claims of communism and its leader's promise of a better world. We can now see the problems of many former communist countries. (Refer to any examples of social or environmental problems that have been highlighted recently.) Communism was really a ferocious wolf in sheep's clothing. But there were signs early on: sacrificing individual lives for the so-called good of the state, for example, or denying the existence of God.

'Probably none of us want to get taken in like that. One thing we can do is to pray that God will give us the ability to see that kind of fruit that Jesus is talking about and so know the truth.'

Either leave a few moments of quiet or read the words of Jesus again (Matthew 7:15-20) to close.

8 Money, money, money

Introduction

- **Aim:** To explore if wealth and possessions can bring lasting happiness.
- **Preparation:** Bring to the assembly a pair of sunglasses, an old coat and hat, items of sports equipment (tennis racket, cricket bat), two or three large books, four or five different-sized cardboard boxes.

Content

Select a volunteer to join you at the front. Ask all the pupils to imagine that they had inherited £1000 and to think of the sort of things they would spend it on. Suggest items from the front; a holiday in the Bahamas, some new sports equipment, new clothes, jewellery or a new watch, books, a midi hi-fi system, a computer, a portable TV, a video recorder, a CD player etc.

Pause after you make each suggestion and ask the volunteer to hold or wear one of the items you have brought with you; the sunglasses, cricket bat and tennis racket, coat and hat, books and the empty boxes. Write the names of your suggestions clearly on the side of each box; portable TV, video recorder etc. The aim of the activity is to get the volunteer fully loaded and struggling to balance the boxes and other items. If any drop, pick them up and give them back to the volunteer who remains standing beside you as you explain the application.

Application and response

Explain that you want the pupils to think about their attitude to money and possessions. Go on by saying money is important: most people use it to buy the necessities of life – food to eat, clothes to keep warm and somewhere to live. However, it's easy to fall into the trap of thinking, 'I wish I had more money,' or, 'I wish I could buy that new ...,' and some people really believe that if they had more money all their problems would be solved.

Pause, and continue with something along these lines:

'If that were true,why are some of the richest people in the world so unhappy? Some have even been known to lock themselves away and live entirely alone. Why do people who win the football pools sometimes say later (and they often do!) that it was the worst thing that could have ever happened to them, that their wealth has really made them more miserable. The truth is that the love of money can become a real burden!' (Ask your volunteer to drop the items and return to their seat.)

As a further example you may wish to recount the story of Mr. Piet Derksen as outlined in a newspaper article.

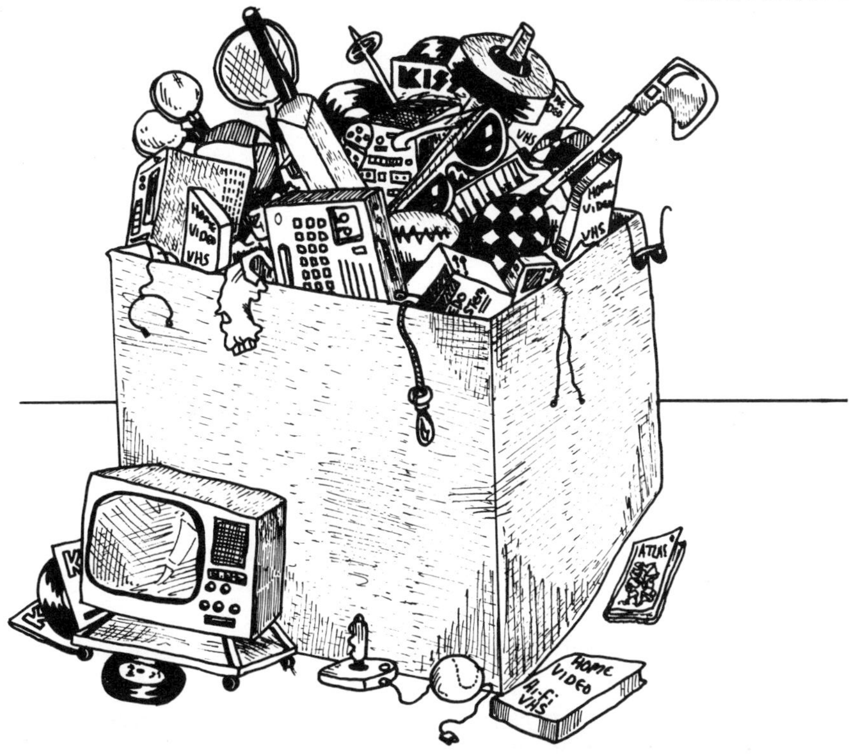

Mr Piet Derksen, one of the wealthiest businessmen in the Netherlands, said he was selling his sports equipment business and giving about £107 million to finance Third World projects. Mr Derksen, a devout Catholic, said: 'My wealth has been like a stone around my neck – I'm glad to get rid of it. I could shout with joy.'

The Apostle Paul said this,

What did we bring into the world? Nothing! What can we take out of the world? Nothing! So then, if we have food and clothes, that should be enough for us. But those who want to get rich fall into temptation and are caught in the trap of many foolish and harmful desires, which pull them down to ruin and destruction. For the love of money is the source of all kinds of evil (1 Timothy 6:7–10a).

Explain that Paul wasn't saying that to have money is wrong, but to love money and be greedy for more can only spoil a person's life.

Finish with the questions: 'Do you think to be rich would really make you happy or do you think there are more important things in life? What do you think they are?'

9 Peace and war

Introduction

- **Aim:** To explore the cause of war and conflict and to examine the Christian belief that conflict stems from the human heart.
- **Preparation:** Cardboard boxes from a local supermarket with one of the words jealousy / envy / pride / insecurity / hatred / selfishness / prejudice / greed written on one side. Do not let the pupils see the words.

Content

Read out a recent news story about a war or conflict (unfortunately these should not be hard to find) or summarise a recent TV news bulletin. Explain that in the last 45 years there have been over 100 wars/ conflicts in many different countries: eg Cuba, Chile, Cyprus, Israel, Lebanon, Nigeria, Afghanistan, Vietnam, Korea, Yugoslavia, Ethiopia, Hungary, Uganda, Iran, Iraq, Falkland Islands etc.

Continue with something along these lines:

'So what is it that causes all these wars? The Apostle Paul wrote: "What human nature does is quite plain... People become enemies and they fight; they become jealous, angry and ambitious. They separate into parties and groups..." (Galatians 5:19,20).'

Application and response

Ask one of the pupils to build a wall with the boxes on the stage, with the words facing the audience. As this happens explain that all these things build a wall between people, cause barriers and can create conflict.

Now ask your volunteer to read Ephesians 2:14, and as you explain it demonstrate the truth of that verse, pushing the wall over. Ask the pupils if they have had an argument with somebody already today and point out that that's the kind of thing that builds walls between people. Explain that Christians believe that Jesus came to knock down those kind of walls between people and to bring peace between you and others and between you and God.

Close with a prayer for people involved in a current conflict (which young people will be aware of) and also drawing out the point about understanding and dealing with the things which cause conflict and anger in our own lives.

I know a man who can...

Introduction

- **Aim:** To explore the idea that in order to make the right choices in life we need expert help.

Content

Select four volunteers to play the game Rock, Scissors, Paper. Ask them to pair off and face their partners with left palms open flat, and right hands made into fists. As you shout out the signals 1,2,3, everyone acts together. On 1 and 2 each person hits his palm with his fist. On 3 he either keeps his hand in a fist (symbolising a rock), points out his index and middle fingers (scissors), or opens it flat (paper). Depending on the symbol his partner forms, a person wins, loses, or ties. The rules are as follows: rock smashes scissors (scissors lose); scissors cuts paper (paper loses); paper covers rock (rock loses). Start as a 'best of three' competition: the winners then play each other. When the winner is found give him a choice of two small prizes.

Application and response

'That was a simple game about making choices. We all make lots of choices every day: what to have for breakfast, what clothes to wear, what sweets to buy, what music to listen to, what TV programmes to watch, whether or not to do our homework. Sometimes we make bigger and more important choices: Will I lie or tell the truth? Will I be hurtful or kind? How will I treat other people? Will I smoke or not? What sort of job will I do when I leave school? Some choices are small, some are very big and we need to think carefully, but its important to make the right choice because our choices affect the way we live.

'In the Bible Jesus talked about the kind of choices he wanted people to make about all sorts of things – about forgiving people who have hurt us, about helping the poor and needy, about the way we use our money, about our relationships with friends and parents, and the importance of making the right choice.' At this point it would be helpful to give an example from your own personal experience of a choice you have made as a Christian and how the Bible and prayer have helped in the making of that choice.

'The question is: Who are we going to listen to when we make our choices? It's your choice!'

11 Fixed on Jesus

Introduction

- **Aim:** To suggest to pupils that what they will achieve in life depends on whose example they are following.

Content

Get eight volunteers and place them in pairs at the front of the hall. They should stand face to face, arms outstretched in front of them, palms to their partner's palms. Ask them to close their eyes and drop their hands to their sides. Now, with eyes still closed, bring their palms up and find the other person's again. Drop hands again. Keeping eyes closed, turn around three times and try to touch palms again. Now look straight at their partners and touch palms again. The volunteers can then return to their seats.

Application and response

'If you want to be successful at doing something, it's important that you keep your eyes fixed on what you want to do.' Give some examples, like: what do you think might happen if you are cutting something with a sharp knife without looking – you might chop your finger off!

'Its important to keep your eyes fixed on the road when you are riding a bike to avoid holes in the road and other road users! In a sprint race the really good runners keep their eyes fixed on the finishing tape, and their heads never move until they have finished the race.

'There was a writer in the Bible who reminded fellow Christians that to go in the right direction in life they needed to keep their eyes fixed on Jesus (Hebrews 12:2). Christians today believe that they need to keep their attention on Jesus and follow his example.' Give an illustration from your own experience about how following Christ's example has helped you go in the right direction in life, or use this one.

6th-form college student Clynt Wright tells how alcohol had become his escape from a difficult home situation. 'Life was a bit of a shambles, really, a bit sad. I was deeply depressed and almost an alcoholic. I had always believed in God to some extent, but thought that had nothing to do with me.' A conversation on board a cross-channel ferry on the way to a ski-ing holiday made Clynt think again and he soon decided to become a follower of Jesus. 'I know it sounds stereotyped,' says Clynt a year later, 'but now there does seem to be a meaning to life, there seems to be hope. I know I'll always come out of the troubles. I suppose Jesus has taken it all off my back.'

'The question is: Whose example do you want to follow in life? What direction are you hoping to be going in?'

12 Under the skin

Introduction

- **Aim:** To help pupils understand the value of empathising with others.

Content

Tell the group you are going to do an exercise in getting into someone else's skin. All they have to do is to think of answers to your questions. (For greater impact get two volunteers out the front to provide answers, but give the option of 'passing' on any question to avoid embarrassment.

1. Think of one thing that makes you very happy.
2. Think of one thing that makes you very sad.
3. Think of one thing that makes you angry.
4. Think of one thing that makes you frightened.

Now ask the group to imagine they are a well-known soap-opera character. Suggest a couple of names, but they can think of another if they prefer. Ask the same four questions.

So far this should have been fun! Tell the group you are going to do it one more time, and you want them to do it seriously. (If you have volunteers out the front, allow them to return to their seats before this section.) Ask them to think of someone they don't like – warn them not to say the name out loud – and to imagine they are that person. Ask the same four questions.

Application and response

'What is it like to be in someone else's skin? To think like they do, feel like they do? Of course we can only imagine it.

'There is a lot of misunderstanding in the world, a lot of hurt, a lot of fighting, because we only look at things from our own point of view. We don't take time to consider what the other person is thinking, to imagine how they feel. The word for that is selfishness – only thinking of ourselves.

'The apostle Paul, writing to a church in a city called Philippi, suggested an answer to this selfishness. He said, "Look out for one another's interests, not just your own." Then he pointed people to the example of Jesus.' (Read Philippians 2:5–8.)

'Jesus actually got into human skin to share our lives with us, to feel as we do. We can't literally get into another person's skin, but we can imagine what it is like. Perhaps if we do that we won't find we have quite so much reason to dislike that person we each thought of earlier.'

13 Invisible people

Introduction

- **Aim:** To challenge pupils to think about those who are most often ignored in society.
- **Preparation:** You will need: a lab. coat, a pair of gloves, a paper bag to go over your head, and a suitable 'potion' (coloured soft drink) in a glass. Rehearse the content so that you can really get into the 'mad scientist' role. It could also be played by two people: one the scientist (you) and the other (a pupil volunteer) the subject who becomes invisible.

Content

Introduce yourself as a brilliant scientist who has discovered the long sought-after secret of invisibility. Explain that in this assembly the pupils are going to be privileged to be at a world first: you are going to make yourself invisible by drinking the 'potion'.

When you have drunk it, quickly explain that to avoid horrifying everyone with your disappearance you will cover your head and hands. Put on the gloves and place the paper bag over your head (no skin must show). Describe becoming invisible and then the feeling of reappearing (whilst you still have the bag and gloves on).

After 'reappearing' remove the bag and gloves. Ask who believes that you became invisible? Presumably no one. Now ask if anyone believes that it is possible to become invisible? Of course not.

Application and response

Allow the mood to become more serious and explain it *is* possible to become invisible by becoming old, or ill or poor. Continue with something along these lines:

'It's easy to forget the old, trapped in their own homes; or to forget the ill, out of sight in hospitals; or to forget the starving, apart from special appeals. All of these people are there all the time, but we often do not see them – it's just as if they were invisible.' (Read Matthew 25:34–40.)

'Jesus was saying that if we want to live God's way it also involves helping others in need, about looking after the "invisible people" and providing help in practical ways. Not just when we see an appeal on the TV but all the time.'

You may wish to go on and briefly highlight an example of how Christians are working locally, nationally or internationally to meet the needs of others as an expression of God's love for the world. Or encourage pupils to get involved in community or school projects helping some of these 'invisible people'.

14 Facing the future

Introduction

- **Aim:** To encourage pupils to consider that God is someone who they can trust with their future.
- **Preparation:** You will need to prepare four cards with a large letter T on one side and a large letter F on the other.

Content

Explain that you are going to start with a quiz and select four volunteers to help you. Give each volunteer a True/False card. Continue by saying that almost every day people are inventing things which are supposed to help us in the future. The quiz is about discoveries or inventions which may be appearing soon in this country. The volunteers have to vote if they think the discovery or invention is true (T) or if it's just made up (F). (In fact all are true although a certain amount of incredulity from yourself should help to confuse the volunteers.)

Select three or four of the illustrations below for your assembly. The paragraph in bold is the question, after which the volunteers can vote. The following paragraph is then read aloud to confirm the discovery or invention.

1. The walking TV?

A scientist is developing a television with robot legs so that it can move freely from room to room. At night it patrols the house and sounds an alarm if the built-in security camera detects an intruder.

The ANIMAN, a walking robot TV built by design student Brian Elliot, also becomes the ANISCOUT when night falls, patrolling the home and sounding an alarm if an intruder is detected. The Sony Corporation hope to develop the invention and plan to add voice recognition as one of its features.

2. The grass lawn that weeds itself?

A gardener's dream come true! A Canadian scientist has discovered a type of grass that can grow in any kind of soil, that doesn't need fertiliser or watering, while at the same time killing any weeds which grow around it.

Dr Jan Weijer, a geneticist of the University of Alberta, has discovered a grass growing in the Rocky Mountains that produces it's own natural herbicide, which destroys or slows down plant growth around the grass. Marketing of this new grass to gardeners should begin in the next few years.

3. Fizzy milk?

The American United Dairy Industry Association is planning to launch carbonated 'fizzy' milk to be marketed alongside Coke, Pepsi, and 7-Up. Flavours in development so far include peach, banana, cola and rum.

It's true. The drink will have a skimmed milk base (all of the calcium, most of the vitamins and minerals, but none of the fat) to which the fizz and flavourings are added. Strangely enough, fizzy milk doesn't taste anything like real milk. If it's unflavoured it tastes like soda water; if its flavoured it tastes like a fruit drink.

4. Car satellite navigation?

By the end of the decade motor cars will contain satellite navigation systems which will be able to pinpoint the car's position anywhere in the world, as well as warn you of approaching bad weather.

Nissan of Japan is spearheading a Satellite Drive Information device and your exact position will be shown on the car's computer display screen. The picture will be transmitted via satellite and will even tell you where to make turns and avoid traffic jams.

5. Toilet that takes your temperature?

Here is the ultimate answer for all hypochondriacs: a Japanese toilet company has produced an 'intelligent loo' which provides information on your health every time you use it.

Toto Ltd, Japan's largest manufacturer of sanitary ware, is thinking of marketing an intelligent toilet which takes your temperature and blood pressure, analyses 'certain substances' and weighs you every time you use it. It is hoped that patients 'on the loo' can be monitored by their doctor via a telecommunication link to the doctor's surgery.

Application and response

'It's amazing the things people invent to try to make our lives more comfortable in the future. Who knows what will be next, things are moving so quickly? When your grandparents were younger could they have guessed that a man would walk on the moon? Could they have ever imagined cooking in a microwave? I wonder if you can imagine what you will be doing in the future?

'Many people try to find out what the future holds for them. Not knowing what might happen in the future is a real worry to some people. Perhaps you have wished you knew what lies ahead, but the truth is that even though we can try, no one here really knows what will happen in the future.'

Share from your experience that even though you don't know what the future holds, as a Christian you believe that God knows. He is in control. Because you know he loves you, you can trust him with the whole of your life. Go on to explain that for Christians, trusting in God each day brings security and optimism and peace of mind not only about that day but for facing the future as well.

15 Death – the beginning?

Introduction

- **Aim:** To explain what Christians believe about death and beyond.
- **Preparation:** You will ned two toilet rolls and two prizes.

Content

Mummy Wrap Game: Select two pairs of volunteers (each pair should be same sex). Provide one member of each pair with a toilet roll and tell them to make an Egyptian mummy out of their partner. Allow three minutes for the activity. The winning couple is the best covered mummy with no skin or clothing left showing. Award a prize to the winner.

Application and response

'Mummification was the ancient Egyptian method of burying the dead, and the kings and leaders were usually buried with all their possessions (and servants) ready for their new existence in the after life. That was one belief about life after death and today, in the 20th century, people have all sorts of different ideas about what happens after death.

'A philosopher once said: "Everything that happens in this world happens at the time God chooses. He sets the time for birth and the time for death" (Ecclesiastes 3:1–2). In other words the philosopher believed that God has a purpose for every life and the circumstances of life and death are under his control.

'Hundreds of years later Jesus went on to say: "I am the resurrection and the life. Whoever believes in me will live, even though he dies" (John 11:26).

'Christians believe in eternal life, promised by God to those who believe in him, and that death when it comes can be faced in the knowledge that it is a doorway into another life with God, which goes on for ever.

'Film star Steve McQueen became a Christian shortly before he died and said, "I expect to win my battle against cancer, but no matter how it goes, I'm at peace with God. I can't lose." He had discovered a friendship with God and the promise of eternal life.

'What do you believe about life after death? Can we really know the truth: are Christians right to trust in Jesus' words, "Whoever believes in me will live, even though he dies"?'

Note: Please be aware that there may be a pupil who has been recently bereaved. This may require sensitivity and a careful choice of words. Check with the head teacher or member of staff responsible for the assembly before you start.

Receiving and giving

16

Introduction

- **Aim:** To encourage pupils to be generous in their actions to others.

Content

Ask who has ever needed a blood transfusion, perhaps after an accident or an operation. Then ask the pupils if they have ever heard of Dr Charles Drew.

'Charles Drew was a doctor and surgeon, a black American, who discovered how to treat blood so that it could be stored until needed. At the beginning of World War II the British Government invited him to England to set up blood banks there. Thousands of lives were saved as a result. There may even be someone sitting here today whose grandfather's life was saved by a blood transfusion during the war.

'Several years later, in 1950, Dr Drew was in a car accident. Seriously injured, he needed blood to save his life. He was rushed to the nearest hospital, but this hospital refused to admit him because he was black and gave directions to the nearest hospital for blacks. He died before they could get him there.'

Application and response

'How sad that a man who had given the world such a valuable gift should himself be refused it because of prejudice.

'Whether or not we have had a blood transfusion, each one of us has benefited in thousands of different ways from the discoveries of people like Charles Drew. How many times have we been like that hospital and shut the door on people in need? When did we last see someone who was upset or being bullied or needing help and we ignored them?

'Jesus talked about caring for the hungry, the sick, the lonely and those in trouble, and said that every time we do something for them it is like doing it for him. We have been given so much, let's be generous in giving to others. We never know whom we may be helping. Or whom we are shutting the door on.'

ALL ABOUT FEELINGS

17 Head over heart

Introduction

- **Aim:** To introduce the subject of emotions and to present some biblical advice on dealing with them.
- **Preparation:** Copy the sentences on the right onto pieces of paper or card.

Content

Announce that you are going to try a little drama exercise and that you need ten volunteers who have some acting ability. Give each one a card and tell them that, one at a time, you are going to ask them to read out the sentence on it putting as much feeling into it as they can. This is an exercise to see how good they are at portraying emotions.

These sentences, or similar, are written on the cards. Some have extra information in brackets to help in portraying the emotion.

'I feel really depressed.' (It's the first Monday of term!)

'I'm scared silly.' (It's your first job interview.)

'Stand back, I'm coming through!' (Arnie, The Terminator!)

'I hate him.'

'I love him.'

'I'll get my own back if it's the last thing I do!' (Bitterness)

'I feel really great.' (You have scored the winning goal/run/basket.)

'I want to hide.' (You have just broken the head's office window.)

'Wow!' (You have just won the pools.)

'I've lost my teddy bear.' (It's the end of the world for a three year old.)

Application and response

'Emotions are part of our everyday life. At the extremes they may make us laugh or cry, but most of the time they just leave us feeling either good or churned up. We may sometimes wish we did not have them, but Christians believe our emotions are God-given. That is true of all our feelings, not only love, but anger and hate as well. The Bible tells us that Jesus got so angry at the money-changers who were exploiting the people who came to the Temple in Jerusalem that he threw their tables over and drove them out with a home-made whip. He was rightly angry and took some courageous action as a result.

'The thing about emotions is that we need to make sure "our heads stay in control". Emotions don't know the difference between right and wrong. Our minds usually do. Emotions can spur us on to doing either something brave or something foolish. Our minds have to decide which is which.

'King David had some good advice in one of his songs, which is written in the Bible. One line in the song says: "In your anger do not sin; when you are on your beds, search your hearts and be silent" (Psalm 4:4). In other words, don't always react to the way you feel at the time; sleep on it and give it some thought. That way you are more likely to do something constructive than something harmful. If you think about it, that's good advice!'

Note: If you are using this as an introduction to other talks on feelings, tell the pupils that you will be going on to look specifically at some other emotions in the near future.

18 It makes sense!

Introduction

- **Aim:** To show pupils that there is an answer to the confusion and uncertainty that many feel.
- **Preparation:** Photocopy SENSE from this book onto an OHP acetate and cut it into pieces along the dotted lines. Spread the pieces on an OHP ready for the assembly.

Content

Ask who likes puzzles and get a volunteer to do an eight piece puzzle. Switch on the OHP and tell him that he has 90 seconds to arrange the pieces to make sense. Give no further explanation.

After the 90 seconds, assuming he has failed, tell him that if he follows the instructions you are going to give him, it will make sense. The instructions are: Arrange the pieces in descending order from 8 on the left to 1 on the right and turn all the odd-numbered pieces upside-down. Now it makes SENSE!

Application and response

'The world can seem a very confusing place. All around us we see a mixture of good and evil, of beauty and ugliness. Then we look inside ourselves and find that same mixture of good and evil, beauty and ugliness. It is not surprising that we sometimes feel confused and find it difficult to make sense of what life's really all about.

'But the good news is that there is help available. Take the story of Jesus. In his teaching and healing, people saw tremendous goodness and beauty. In his trial and crucifixion there was awful evil and ugliness. His friends were thrown into fear and confusion. Then Jesus appeared to them again.' (You could briefly describe the encounter on the Emmaus Road in Luke 24:13–35.) 'He showed them how what had happened all fitted together. It wasn't just chance. It made sense. Instead of confusion, depression and anger, the disciples were filled with peace and joy. That is still true today. People all over the world, from every kind of background, are still discovering that the story of Jesus makes sense of life.'

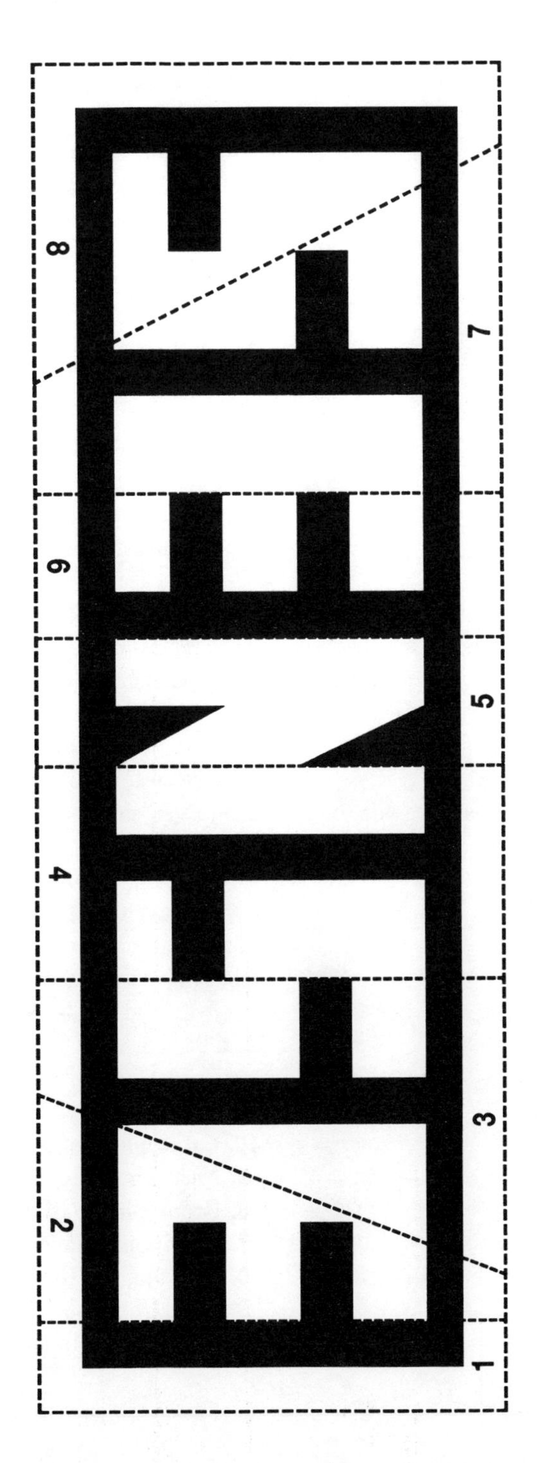
SENSE
1
2
3
4
5
6
7
8

19 Facing fear

Introduction

- **Aim:** To show that fear can have a negative influence on our lives and that security overcomes fear. The assembly also introduces the Christian belief that only in God can people find real and lasting security.
- **Preparation:** An OHP acetate with the top ten phobias, as listed below.

Content

Ask the pupils what sort of things they are afraid of: you may also use any personal stories of things which bother you – heights, exams, Alton Towers amusement rides!

What is fear? The dictionary says it's 'an unpleasant emotion caused by coming danger. To be afraid'. Continue with something like:

'It's interesting that sometimes things which don't bother us can make other people really afraid. Often our own experiences can also make us afraid (being bitten by a dog as a child can cause people to be afraid of dogs for the rest of their lives).' Point out that sometimes fear can be a good thing, for example, the fear of being run over makes us more safety conscious when crossing the road.

'When fear really grips a person it is known as a 'phobia' – eg xenophobia, the fear of meeting strangers – and it can ruin peoples lives. Researchers have discovered what the top ten fears are....' Pause and ask the pupils to think about what fears they think reached the top ten.

Give the top ten fears in reverse order from the previously prepared OHP acetate:

10. Cardiophobia (heart disease)
9. Necrophobia (dead bodies)
8. Brontophobia (thunderstorms)
7. Carcinophobia (cancer)
6. Hypsophobia (heights)
5. Claustrophobia (confined spaces)
4. Agoraphobia (open spaces)

3. **Aerophobia (flying)**
2. **Sociophobia (people)**
1. **Arachnophobia (spiders)**

Explain that sometimes people can develop a 'phobia' or terrible fear about some very unusual things. We might think alektorophobia (fear of chickens), linonophobia (fear of string) and triskaidekaphobia (fear of the number 13) are funny, but for the person concerned it can be a real problem.

Application and response

'How do people overcome fear? When they feel secure, when they know they are safe from danger, when they can trust in something or someone who is certain not to fail. Christians believe that trusting in God provides real security, they believe that God loves us and that his love is more powerful than any fears or worries than can ruin our lives (1 John 4:18).' Give a personal example from your own experience or use Psalm 91:1–6, explaining that it's a poem by someone who really knew what it was like to trust God.

20 Blow up!

Introduction

- **Aim:** To show that unchecked anger can not only hurt others, but also spoil our own lives.
- **Preparation:** Bring three or four balloons to the assembly.

Content

Select two or three 'brave and fearless' volunteers to join you at the front. Give each a balloon and ask them to blow it up, and keep blowing until it bursts! If a volunteer 'backs out', don't worry, there will always be one who goes for the burst! Encourage applause for the volunteers.

Application and response

Referring to the 'balloon bursting' illustration, ask the pupils: 'Have you ever felt like that? Sometimes we get so annoyed, so angry, that we just can't hold it back any longer until...BANG!..we explode, and all the anger comes pouring out. Usually we say things we regret, we do things we wish we hadn't, we get out of control. We hurt other people and we hurt ourselves. You see our anger doesn't just

damage other people but it can also spoil our own lives as well.

'Sometimes people "bottle up" their anger inside. They might have been angry about something or another person for years and although they might have even forgotten what they were angry about to start with, the feeling is just eating away inside them and ruining their life.'

Explain that Christians believe that God inspired the Bible to be written to help us live our lives to the full. 'It's full of practical and sensible advice for ordinary people like you and me. It shows us how to stop our lives being spoilt by emotions like anger which, if unchecked, can become just like a disease and destroy a person's life. Here are three simple pieces of advice from the Bible.' Encourage the pupils to think about these verses.

'If you stay calm, you are wise, but if you have a hot temper, you only show how stupid you are' (Proverbs 14: 29).

'Everyone must be quick to listen, but slow to speak and slow to become angry' (James 1:19).

'Do not use harmful words, but only helpful words, the kind that build up and *provide what is needed* (encourage), so that what you say will *do good to* (help) those who hear you' (Ephesians 4:29). (You may wish to paraphrase this verse using the words in brackets.)

Explain that Christians believe that if we want him to, God can help us to put this advice into practice in our lives. Conclude with:

'In a few moments of quiet ask yourself the questions: Are you angry with someone? What do you think you should do about it? Should you ask God to help you?'

Note: You may wish to explain in the application that it's not always wrong to get angry. We may feel anger at injustice in the world, the plight of starving people in Africa or young people living homeless in some of our towns and cities. But we should allow it to motivate us into action to bring about the end of such injustice.

21 Another fine mess...

Introduction

Aim: To show that even though we may want to give up when we fail, God never gives up on us.

Content

Select and read three of the following humorous stories of people who failed:

• As part of his act while appearing in Roberts Brothers' Circus at Southend in August 1978, Janos the Incredible Rubber man was lowered to the floor hanging from a trapeze, with his legs wrapped somewhere behind his head. Normally, he rolls around for a time to the applause of amazed audiences, before reverting to a more normal human posture. On this occasion he just sat there. 'I couldn't move,' he said later, by way of explanation. The situation was resolved by a circus official, Mr Kenneth Julian. 'We put Janos in the back of my van and took him to hospital.' Doctors wrestled with the problem for thirty minutes and ordered the Incredible Rubber Man to lie flat for a week.

• The most unsuccessful hijack attempt ever made took place in 1976. On a flight across America the hijacker rose from his seat, drew a gun and took the stewardess hostage. 'Take me to Detroit,' he said. 'We're already going to Detroit,' she replied. 'Oh ... good,' he said, and sat down again.

• In 1971 Mr and Mrs Farmer of Margate travelled to Wales for their summer holidays. At the start of the week they joined a British Rail mystery tour. It went to Margate. 'We were expecting the Welsh Mountains,' they said afterwards. 'We nearly fell through the platform,' said Mr. Farmer, who had been looking forward to getting away all the summer. Declining a tour of the town, Mr and Mrs Farmer popped home tor a cup of tea.

• After weeks of extremely careful planning, seventy-five convicts completely failed to escape from Saltillo Prison in Northern Mexico. In November 1975 they had started digging a secret tunnel designed to bring them up at the other side of the prison wall. On the 18th of April 1976, guided by pure genius, their tunnel

came up in the nearby courtroom in which many of them had been sentenced. The surprised judges returned all seventy-five to jail.

- **In the early 1970s Mrs Helen Ireland of Auburn in California failed her driving test in the first second. She got into the car, said 'Good morning' to the driving instructor and started the engine. However, she mistook the accelerator for the clutch and shot straight through the wall of the Driving Test Centre.**

Application and response

'Everybody gets it wrong sometimes, perhaps not like the funny stories we've just heard, but we have let a friend down and they're not speaking to us, we've failed an exam and we feel terrible, or we've let ourselves down when we did something we were especially trying not to do. Feeling a failure is not very nice, and sometimes we just want to give up because we think we've blown it and there's nothing we can do.

'In the Bible there is the story of one of Jesus' disciples who felt just like that. He was called Peter and he really got it wrong. He let his friends down, he let himself down and he let Jesus down. He ran away when Jesus was arrested, he denied he even knew Jesus when he thought people might recognise him. He actually broke down and wept when he realised what a total failure he was. If we had known him we would have probably wanted nothing more to do with him.

'But amazingly the Bible tells us that despite all that had happened in Peter's life, when Jesus appeared to his disciples (after he had been raised from the dead) he didn't give up on Peter and treat him like some sort of outcast. Instead he forgave him, encouraged him and even instructed him to be a leader among the first Christians. Peter put his failure behind him and became a great and courageous leader in the early church.'

Ask the pupils to consider this thought: 'Even when other people give up on us, even when we feel a total failure ourselves, Christians believe that Jesus never gives up, he helps us to start again, because he wants the very best for our lives.'

22 Waist-high waste

Introduction

- **Aim:** To show that guilt can be a kind of pollution within us which needs dealing with just as much as the build-up of waste and pollution in the world around us.
- **Preparation:** You will need scissors, old newspapers, potatoes, a potato-peeler, a bowl of soapy water, clean socks and a towel. And make sure you wear socks!

Content

Ask for three volunteers to help you with some everyday tasks. Set one to cutting headlines from the newspapers and one to peeling potatoes. Give the third the bowl of soapy water. Then take your socks off, hold your nose and drop the socks into the water and ask the third volunteer to wash them for you.

Ask the three volunteers what they are going to do with the discarded paper, the potato peelings and the dirty water. Thank them and say that you will deal with the waste. Send them back to their seats.

Ask all the pupils to imagine that they are in a sealed room. There are enough supplies of air, food and drink, but no way to get rid of the waste. Picture the build-up of rubbish, the awful smell, the disease and death that would result.

Fortunately, planet Earth has it's own clever waste-disposal and recycling systems, such as the bacteria that digest dead plant and animal matter, recycling the nutrients back into the ecosystem.

Application and response

'There is another kind of waste and that is a waste which we all produce within us. It is when we hurt others or other people hurt us. Anger, jealousy, bitterness, guilt – all these things build up inside us and begin to create a 'bad smell'. It is now well established that such feelings can actually cause physical illness if they continue for any length of time.

'Fortunately, God has provided us with a way of dealing with this rubbish, a kind of 'sin-disposal' system. It is called forgiveness. When we ask forgiveness for the wrongs we have done, and forgive those who have hurt us, that rubbish gets cleaned out.' (You may wish to illustrate this point with a practical illustration of forgiving others, either from personal experience or a recent newspaper / TV story.) 'One of Jesus' disciples put it like this: "If we confess our sins to God, he will keep his promise and do what is right: he will forgive us our sins and purify us from all our wrongdoing" (1 John 1:9).'

Suggest that in a few moments of quiet, pupils might like to use God's sin-disposal system by forgiving others or asking for forgiveness themselves.

23 Hidden strength

Introduction

- **Aim:** To explore the confidence and security that comes from the 'inner strength' God gives to individuals who believe in and follow him.
- **Preparation:** You will need some raw eggs and an apron. Practice this at home first to convince yourself it works!

Content

Start off the assembly by asking the pupils who their favourite sports personalities are. You need examples from sports where being fitter and stronger makes you better, such as football, boxing, athletics. Having established that more muscle is a good thing for many sports, ask for someone good at sports to come to the front to help you in the next part of the assembly. Explain that you want them to use their strength to break a raw egg.

You may well know that if you try to crush an egg using both your hands clasped, with fingers locked together, with the egg lying end to end in each of the palms of your hands, then no matter how hard you squeeze you won't be able to break it. (Given that things don't always go according to plan equip the volunteer

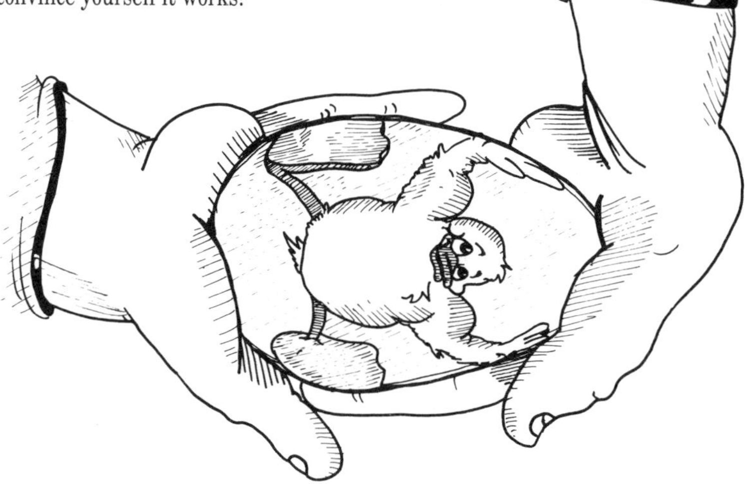

with an apron. Have a spare egg to hand as well! If the egg breaks it is because it moved in the palm of the volunteer and did not remain end to end facing the pressure.)

Application and response

With the egg still whole explain why it has survived. Although an egg has a very fragile shell that is easily cracked it can withstand the pressure because of its hidden strength – produced by its shape and the way it is put together. Explain that as long as the egg lies end to end not even Frank Bruno could smash it.

Conclude with something along these lines:

'It's easy to think that strength is only to do with how many bulging muscles you have or how much you look like Arnold Schwarzenegger. But many sportsmen and women have found another strength deep inside them, a hidden strength, a strength of character which comes from knowing God.

'Carl Lewis, winner of many gold medals for track and field events, said after the 1984 Olympics in Los Angeles, "I've had a great career and of course a great summer of Olympics." (He won four gold medals.) "1984 was probably the most trying year of my life inside and outside the track. More than any other year, I realised how important Jesus Christ was to my life. In the weeks of the Olympics, I realised there was no way I could exist without him."

'Kriss Akabusi, one of Britain's outstanding athletes, said: "I may come back from the Olympics a champ or a chump, but the most important thing is that Jesus is real in my life, whether I win or lose."

'Athlete Jonathan Edwards has competed for England in the triple jump. He is a Christian and refuses to compete on Sundays. "I've got an assurance deep down in my heart that God's there and that I know I'm important to him. I've seen God look after me. I've seen his work in my life." That sort of assurance is what gives inner strength.'

At the end of the assembly you could break the egg to show that it was raw and not hard-boiled.

24 Positively healthy

Introduction

- **Aim:** To encourage a positive approach to life and to show that this is also the Christian approach.
- **Preparation:** You will need four sets of cards marked A and B for volunteers to display.

Content

Ask for volunteers to do a magazine-type personality test and select four to come out. Give them each a pair of cards and explain that you are going to give them three everyday situations plus two possible ways of reacting to each situation. They are to think which way they would be most likely to react and hold up the appropriate card. Ask the rest of the assembly to think about which way they would react.

Situation 1. You have just done rather badly in a test. Are you more likely to say:

A. It was a hard test and I hadn't done enough revision, but I'll do better next time.

or

B. I'm not particularly good at that subject and I don't think I ever will be.

Situation 2. You were playing sport last weekend and had a poor match. Are you more likely to say:

A. I had an off day but I hope to be back on form next week.

or

B. I don't think this is really my game

and I would be better to give it up.

Situation 3. You have just had a really nasty family argument. Are you more likely to say:

A. We were all in a bad mood, but it will soon blow over and things will be okay.

or

B. We are never going to get on in our family and the sooner I leave home the better.

Ask everyone, volunteers and audience, to put up their hands if they got two or three As, and then similarly for two or three Bs. Thank your volunteers, who can return to their seats.

Application and response

'The A answers in each case were more optimistic. Optimists say, "That was a one-off situation. There was a good reason for it. Next time will be better." The B answers were more pessimistic. Pessimists say, "It's my fault – that's the way I am and things are not likely to get any better."

'The interesting thing is that those who think they can do better – the optimists – usually do. In a study of top-class swimmers, for example, the optimists did better when they went back to the pool after a poor performance while the pessimists did worse.

'It also seems to affect our health. Pessimists are more likely to get depressed, in the same way that smokers are more likely to get lung cancer. Pessimists are also more prone to disease as they get older.

'Christians believe they can look at life optimistically. In one of St Paul's letters to a group of the first Christians he says, "We know that in all things God works for good with those who love him, those whom he has called according to his purpose" (Romans 8:28). He was saying that knowing God is in control can enable Christians to be optimistic.

'Did you get more Bs than As? Do you think you are a pessimist? Don't say, "That's the way I am and I can't change." That is just confirming your pessimism! Try saying, "If I think more optimistically, things will actually get better!" Or ask God to show you how he "works for good with those who love him."'

Note: The information for this talk is based on research done by Professor Martin Seligman of the University of Pennsylvania.

25 The parable of the three Cokes

Introduction

- **Aim:** To show the destructive nature of envy and that it is better to be satisfied with what you have.
- **Preparation:** You will need three different sized 'Coke' cups from a cinema or burger bar. Draw three large red clown-type smiles on pieces of card approximately 12cm x 6cm. Write the Manager's questions on three pieces of card. Adapt names and details of the sketch as appropriate and assign the roles of Narrator (N), Manager (M), Abigail (A), Bertha (B) and Chloé (C). Don't forget to rehearse the sketch thoroughly with your helpers / volunteers before the assembly.

Content

N: Once again it is promotion time in the cut-throat world of the burger business. This week international burger giants MacMegaBurger are offering prizes to all customers who can answer two simple questions. Let's hurry down to our local MacMegaBurger to see whether this extra special offer is really drawing them in.

(Enter M and A. A is carrying her 'smile' hidden behind her back.)

M: If you'll just step this way, Miss, I'll ask you your two simple questions. And question number one is: What is your name?

A: Oh, well it's Abigail, actually.

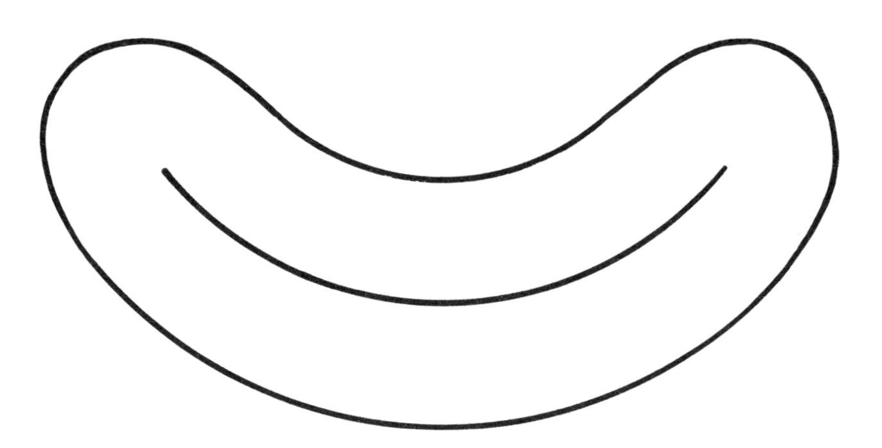

M: Absolutely the right answer! Brilliant! And here comes question number two: Which burger is the best burger in the world?

A: Um, a MacMegaBurger.

M: Congratulations! You have won ... a free Coke! *(Hands her a small Coke. A stands facing front with her Coke and holding her 'smile' up to her lips.)*

N: As we can see, Abigail is very happy with the free drink she has won. And here comes customer number two.

(Enter B)

M: This way, please. Your first question is: What is your name?

B: Um, Bertha.

M: Super! Another correct answer. And question number two is: In a MacMegaBurger Cheeseburger, what do you get beside the famous MacMegaBurger burger?

B: Oh, er, er, ...

M: In a Cheeseburger, besides the burger you get ...

B: Cheese!

M: Wonderful! You have just won ... a medium-sized Coke! *(Hands B a medium Coke. B stands a little to the side of A with her Coke and 'smile'. In exaggerated jerky movements A looks at B's face, B's Coke, then her own Coke. She turns her 'smile' upside-down to become a frown.)*

N: Well, Bertha is obviously very happy with her free drink, but suddenly it looks as though Abigail is somewhat upset. Never mind. Here comes customer number three.

(Enter C)

M: Our lucky third customer this morning. Question number one: What is your name?

C: It's Chloé.

M: A confident answer there. Question number two: In a MacMegaBurger Doubleburger, how many MacMegaBurger prime beef mega two-pounder burgers do you get?

C: Three ... No, no! Two!

M: Correct! Chloé, you have won this giant-sized Coke. *(Hands her a large Coke. C stands between A and B holding up her Coke and 'smile'. A and B repeat the motions as before and both end up looking at C with 'frowns' on their faces.)*

N: Chloé is happy enough, but I'm afraid the other two are rather envious that she has a bigger Coke than they do. In fact, it looks as though there might be trouble here. *(A and B lean forward, look at each other, toss their Coke cups over their shoulders, take hold of C's Coke and turn it upside-down on her head. It could have some liquid in it for greater effect. C turns her 'smile' upside-down and all three face front, displaying 'frowns'.)*

Application and response

'Wanting what someone else has is called envy. Envy is a great destroyer of happiness and a cause of crime and war. That is why in the tenth commandment God tells us not to envy what others have.

'The Bible tells us that St Paul discovered the secret of not letting envy destroy his happiness. He said, "I have learnt to be satisfied with what I have. I know what it is to be in need and what it is to have more than enough. I have learnt this secret, so that anywhere, at any time, I am content" (Philippians 4:11b–12a).

'St Paul had learnt the secret of being content. Perhaps we need to do the same, for our own happiness, and for peace in the world. We're going to be quiet for a moment and if you want to, you can ask God to start to teach us to be satisfied with what we have.'

FESTIVALS

Christmas

ChristmasChristmasCh
ristmasChristmasChrist
masChristmasChristma
sChristmasChristmasC
hristmasChristmasChri
stmasChristmasChrist
masChristmasChristma

26 Christmas unwrapped

Introduction

- **Aim:** To explain that the gifts brought to Jesus by the wise men help us to understand who he is.
- **Preparation:**
  Christmas Team Wrap; two large cardboard boxes (from a local supermarket), Christmas wrapping paper, two pairs of scissors, tape, two ribbon bows, whistle.
  Blindman's Wrap; two cardboard boxes, wrapping paper, tape, two ribbon bows, two blindfolds (scarves).

Content

Comment on the fact that gifts are an important part of Christmas. We all like to receive gifts, but Christmas also provides an opportunity to give gifts to our family, relatives and friends. Ask the pupils to think about the presents they might be buying for their mum, dad, brother, best friend etc ... Explain that in this assembly we are going to practice wrapping a present – but with a few differences. Choose one of the activities below:

Christmas Team Wrap

Select two teams of five or six pupils who stand at one side of the stage. At the other side is placed a large cardboard box for each team with wrapping paper, scissors, tape, ribbon and a bow. Explain that at your signal the first person runs across the stage to the box and begins to wrap it. After 15 seconds a whistle will blow and they must run back to the other side of the stage and be replaced by the next team member who continues the wrapping process. End the relay when everyone on each team has had a turn. Comment on the degree of 'success' of the teams and encourage applause for their efforts.

Blindman's Wrap

Select two volunteers and stand them beside two large boxes of equal size. Give each volunteer some wrapping paper (cut roughly to size), tape or ribbon and a bow (but no scissors). Ask the pupils to wrap up the box, telling them at this point that they must perform the task blindfolded. Comment on the results.

Application and response

Once the activity has ended and the volunteers have returned to their seats, remind the pupils that in the story of the first Christmas the wise men brought some gifts to Jesus. Explain that this part of the story happened some time after the birth of Jesus and the shepherd's visit to the newborn infant (maybe nearly two years later).

Read (or have read by a pupil) Matthew 2:1–12. Continue with something along these lines:

'The gifts brought to Jesus seem to us unusual. When people choose gifts for people they often try to fit the gift to the person they are giving it to.' (Give a personal example of a gift you have given to a friend or relative.) 'The wise men did the same and the gifts they brought help us to understand what they knew about Jesus and the kind of person he was going to be.

Gold was something that was given to kings.

Frankincense was a sweet-smelling resin (gum) used in ceremonies by the priests as they prayed to God for the people.

Myrrh was an expensive spice placed on a body at burial.

'What do you think these gifts tell us about the kind of person Jesus was going to grow up to be and what would happen to him in the future?'

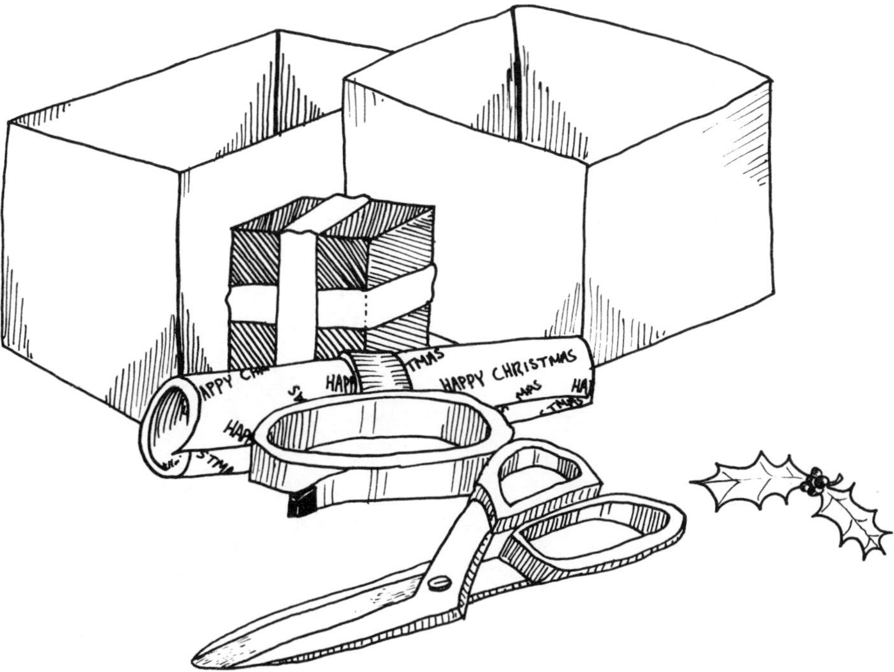

27 What's in a name?

Introduction

- **Aim:** To explain that the names given to Jesus help us to understand who he is.
- **Preparation:** You will need a copy of a book of babies' names, available from most bookshops or stationers.

Content

Ask the pupils if any one knows what their name means. Explain that nearly all of our names have been passed down through history from Latin, Greek, Hebrew or the ancient east and they originally described something about the person who was given the name.

Our names are usually chosen by our parents. They may be names of relatives or grandparents or even a famous person and they make us special and different from other people. Give some examples of common names, ask the pupils with that name to raise their hands before reading out the meaning.

GIRLS

Ann (Hebrew) Full of grace
Emma (Teutonic) A woman of command
Debbie (Hebrew) The bee – an industrious woman who looks for what is sweet in life
Margaret (Latin) A pearl
Rachel (Hebrew) Innocent as a lamb
Sarah (Hebrew) Princess
Susan (Hebrew) Graceful lily
Victoria (Latin) The victorious one

BOYS

Andrew (Greek) Strong and manly
David (Hebrew) The beloved one
George (Greek) The farmer
John (Hebrew) God's gracious gift
Neil (Gaelic) The champion
Paul (Latin) Little
Peter (Latin) The Rock
Robert (Teutonic) A man of brilliant reputation

Application and response

'As we approach Christmas, we might think about the very first Christmas, when a baby called Jesus was born. But what does the name Jesus mean, and how was it chosen? The Bible says it was chosen not by his mother, but was given to him directly by God (the angel told Mary his name was to be Jesus) and his name means "God saves".' (Read Matthew 1:18–23.)

Explain that other titles were also given to this baby (such as Son of the Most High God – Luke 1: 26–33). His name and the other titles all help us to understand how special he is. Emmanuel means 'God is with us'. Conclude with:

What do you think the name Emmanuel tells us about who Jesus really is?'

28 Call my bluff

Introduction

- **Aim:** To suggest that to find out about the real meaning of Christmas we need to look in the Bible and read it for ourselves.
- **Preparation:** Select three of the words from the selection below and on a small filing card write out the three descriptions of each word.

Content

Ask for three volunteers to help you on the 'Call my Bluff' competition. Explain that the quiz is based on an old TV programme where you have to guess the correct meaning of each word. Only one description is the right answer. Give one word with its three descriptions to each volunteer to read out loud. The rest of the pupils are then asked to vote on which they think is the correct answer. Make sure the correct answer (in bold type) is not always the first description.

FALCHION

1. Another name for a ship's wheel
2. A broad curved sword
3. A blindfold used by falconers on their birds of prey

GAZEBO

1. A structure built to provide a view (such as a conservatory on the side of a house)

2. A species of East African antelope
3. A type of boat used on the Great Barrier Reef in Australia

MARIMBA
1. An alcoholic Peruvian drink
2. An African xylophone
3. A lively Spanish dance

FELUCCA
1. A loose woollen cloak worn by Arab men
2. An agricultural tool, like a pickaxe, used in India
3. A small coastal boat used in the Mediterranean

MANGEL-WURZEL
1. A large vegetable, like a beetroot, used as cattle food
2. Another name for a scarecrow
3. An old type of washing machine

Ask if anyone got all the words right.

Application and response

Ask the question, 'Where would you look to find the correct meaning or description of words like the ones we've heard this morning? A dictionary of course – a dictionary helps us to discover the true meaning of a word.' Continue with something along these lines:

'What about a word like Christmas. Well, a dictionary might help, but it doesn't give us a very detailed description of all that Christmas is about. People have all sorts of different ideas; it's a holiday, a chance to visit relatives and friends, eat lots of food, receive presents, watch TV, go to church. But how did it all start? How much do we really know about Christmas? To find the real story behind the word we need to look in the Bible to find out what really happened on the first Christmas.' Read Luke 2:1–7.

Finish by encouraging the pupils to read the rest of the story from the Bible themselves.

29 Good news for all people

Introduction

- **Aim:** To bring the angel's message of the Good News of the birth of Jesus a little nearer home.
- **Preparation:** Enlist a pupil to read Luke 2:8–11. To encourage participation, other pupils could read the sections about different people below.

Content

Begin with the reading of a familiar passage, the announcement of Christ's birth by the angel, Luke 2:8–11. Continue with something along these lines:

'Why was the birth of one baby boy in Palestine nearly two thousand years ago "Good News ... for all the people"? Of course, we are all going to have a holiday and stuff ourselves with food and swop presents, but that is the *celebration* of the news, not the Good News itself. What effect has that birth had on the world that makes it Good News for everyone?

• 'More than eighteen hundred years after that birth, Florence Nightingale went to nurse soldiers wounded in the Crimean War. She went because she was a follower of Jesus and believed she had heard the voice of God telling her she had a mission in life. Florence Nightingale totally revolutionised nursing. Every one of us who has been in hospital has benefited from the tradition she started. That is good news for all people.

• 'Two years after he became a follower of Jesus, William Wilberforce helped found the Anti-Slavery Society. It took forty-eight years of prayer and hard work in Parliament before the Slavery Abolition Act was passed in 1825 – just one month after Wilberforce had died. The end of British involvement in slavery was good news for countless people all over the world.

• 'In the 1950s the Rev Dr Martin Luther King took up the fight against segregation, the separating of people according to the colour of their skin. As a follower of Jesus, he declared that segregation "is a blasphemy and against everything that the Christian religion stands for." By the time he was assassinated in 1968, his voice had been heard around the world. That was good news for all people.'

Application and response

'Whenever a follower of Jesus stands up for the things Jesus stood for – for justice, for truth, for freedom, for care of the poor and needy, for love and forgiveness – that is good news for everyone. Whenever a follower of Jesus stands against the things Jesus stood against – hypocrisy, greed, selfishness, evil of all kinds – that, too, is good news for everyone. Many famous names and countless unknown men and women have changed the world for the better because they were followers of the man who was born in a stable two thousand years ago. Wasn't the angel right when he said that the birth of Jesus was "Good News for all the people"?'

Easter

EasterEasterEasterEas
terEasterEasterEasterE
asterEasterEasterEaste
rEasterEasterEasterEa
sterEasterEasterEaster
EasterEasterEasterEas
terEasterEasterEasterE

30 Power to renew

Introduction

- **Aim:** To suggest that we need the supernatural power which God demonstrated at Easter to tackle the environmental problems of the world.
- **Preparation:** You will need a decent-looking object which can be smashed (such as an odd cup and saucer or a vase), a cloth bag to hold this object (it should be strong enough not to tear when the object is smashed), a hammer, a tube of glue.

Content

Ask who is good at breaking things. Invite a likely character to the front and find out what they have broken recently. Show your breakable object. Give the volunteer a hammer. Say you want him to smash the cup, but to wait a moment as the flying pieces would be dangerous. Put the cup into the bag, make sure you are several feet from the front row, just in case, and get your volunteer to smash it with the hammer. Show one or two of the broken pieces to the audience.

Produce the glue and ask the volunteer if he could stick the pieces back together again to make it as good as new. ... Failing that, is he capable of making a new one? ... Or could he wave a magic wand over the pieces and do a 'Paul Daniels' on them? ... Thank him and ask him to sit down.

Application and response

Breaking things is a one-way process. Mention briefly some of the use of resources and environmental problems which are similarly one-way processes, such as using fossil fuels which cannot be replaced or deforestation which is making animal species extinct. Even where it may be possible to restore things, it can only be at the cost of much determination, scientific research and vast amounts of money. *Naturally*, the possibilities are limited.

But what about *super*naturally? Ask if anyone can think of an occasion in history when something was broken beyond repair and was supernaturally restored?

... What about the resurrection of Jesus? He died on a cross; his heart probably ruptured, literally broken; even the best of today's medicine could not revive that body. But on Easter day he came back to life. Over the next few weeks, hundreds of people saw him. That was supernatural power at work, power from outside our natural universe.

Conclude with something along these lines:

'Listen to what someone who later experienced that power himself said. This is St Paul writing to some other Christians: "This power working in us is the same as the mighty strength which (God) used when he raised Christ from deathl" (Ephesians 1:19–20). He was talking about supernatural power, "working in us".

'People have said that we are quite capable of running the world without God's help. But are we? Look at the mess we are making of it. Perhaps we need the help of the supernatural power which "raised Christ from death"?'

Hold up the bag of broken pieces and shake it.

31 Rotten inheritance

Introduction

- **Aim:** To set wordly riches in perspective and to demonstrate the hope that Easter brings.
- **Preparation:** You will need three boxes containing:

  1. some obviously mouldy bread or rotten fruit;

  2. some worn-out clothing;

  3. an obviously broken toy, cassette recorder or similarly ruined object.

Content

Announce that you are going to tell the story of three people who had a rich uncle who had promised to leave them each something in his will. Ask the pupils to imagine what *they* would like to receive from such a rich uncle, then get three volunteers to play the parts of the inheritors.

- To the **first** nephew/niece the uncle said in his will that he did not want them to go hungry. The solicitor handling the will gave him/her a box with the inheritance. *(Give the first volunteer box number 1, but tell them not to open it yet.)*
- To the **second**, the uncle said he wanted them to be well-dressed. *(Give the second box to the second volunteer with the same instruction.)*
- To the **third**, the uncle said he did not want them to lack for entertainment. *(Third box to third volunteer.)*

Now get each one in turn to open their box and display its contents. Commiserate appropriately, then thank them and send them back to their seats.

Talk about the disappointment, but point out that even if the gifts had been new, that is how they would have ended up eventually. Ask the pupils to remember what they had wished for as an inheritance. Whatever that was, eventually it would wear out or be used up.

Amazingly that is also true of the universe we live in. If you study science you'll eventually learn about the Second Law of Thermodynamics which tells us that the universe is running down. One day it will be like an old battery with no more life left in it.

Application and response

'That may sound all rather depressing. But there was a day in history when things changed; a day when it became possible to hope for things that would never wear out or go rotten. That day was Easter Sunday, the day that Jesus rose from the dead. After that event one of Jesus' closest friends, Peter, could write about "an inheritance that can never perish, spoil or fade – kept in heaven for you" (1 Peter 1:4).

'"An inheritance (a promised gift) that can never perish" – unlike this rotten apple; "that can never ... fade" – unlike these old jeans; "that can never ... spoil" – unlike this broken game. An inheritance that's not part of the universe that is slowly running down, but in heaven.

'It's not wrong to enjoy new things, or to look after them and make them last as long as possible, but eventually they will all wear out. Christians believe that because Jesus rose from the dead on Easter Day it is possible to have an inheritance, which is the promise of a new life to look forward to, that will always remain new and never end.'

32 Mission impossible

Introduction

- **Aim:** To explore the truth of a seemingly impossible event – the Resurrection.
- **Preparation:** Practice the string game at home first, to make sure that you can do it!

Content

Select two pairs of volunteers and give each pair two pieces of string (each about a metre long). One ties one end to his right wrist and the other to his left. His partner repeats the process but, before tying on the second end, crosses his string over his partner's string. The object of the game is to untangle the strings without breaking the string or wriggling the string off the hand.

Solution: To escape, position your partner's string over your forearm and pass the centre of your partner's string through the wrist loop and over your own hand.

Application and response

'It seems impossible, but when the answer is provided, it's easy to understand how to do the game!'

Explain that you are going to read a story (well-known to some) about something which seemed impossible. Read the story of the Resurrection of Jesus from Luke 24: 1–12.

Go on to say that just like the opening activity it seems impossible; who can believe that it really happened? Yet history shows that the tomb was empty. However, still to many people it remains an impossible puzzle. What is the answer? What do you think? (Pause.)

Explain that you have found it only made sense, it only became possible, when you realised and understood that Jesus really was who he said he was!

Finish with the question, 'Who do you think Jesus was? How would that make the impossible, possible?'

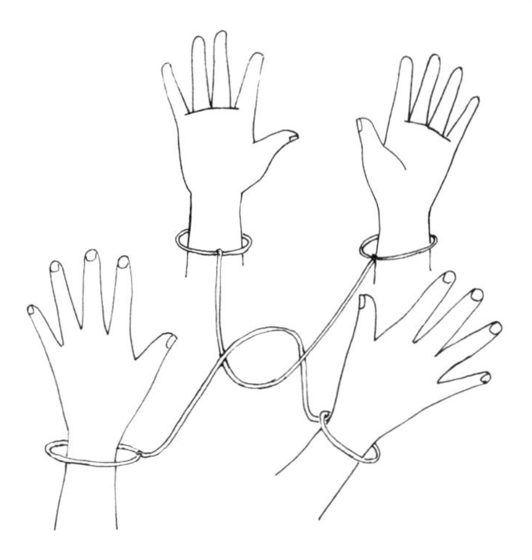

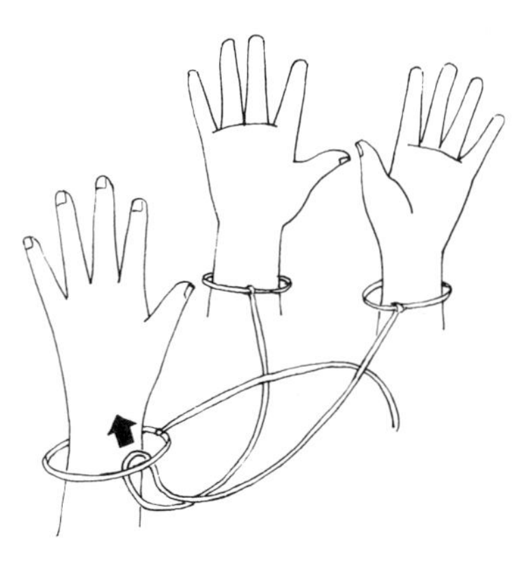

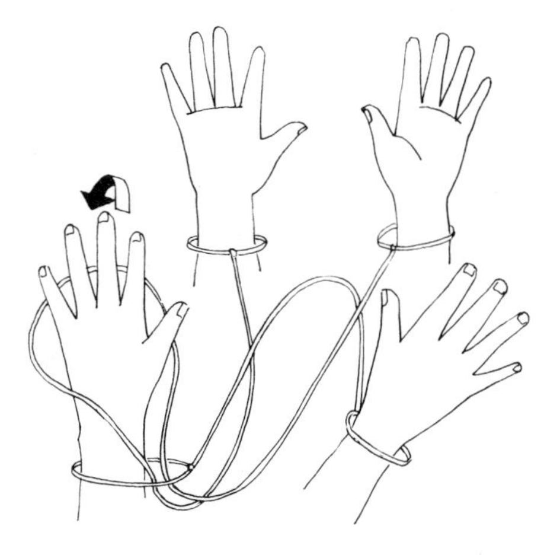

Pentecost

PentecostPentecostPe
ntecostPentecostPente
costPentecostPentecos
tPentecostPentecostPe
ntecostPentecostPente
costPentecostPentecos
tPentecostPentecostPe

33 Pentecost - breath

Introduction

- **Aim:** To illustrate the transforming power of God at Pentecost.
- **Preparation:** A container of bubble liquid is needed.

Content

Ask for a volunteer to come to the front and blow as many bubbles as possible. Then ask all the pupils to think of what made the difference between the slimy liquid in the container and the bubbles, with their perfect shape, their irridescent colours and the lightness that enables them to float in the air? ... Breath. Breath transforms what was dull and earthbound into something beautiful and free.

Application and response

'After Jesus had been crucified, the Bible says the disciples were hiding and frightened for their lives. On the evening of his resurrection, Jesus appeared to them and "he breathed on them" and said, "Receive the Holy Spirit" (John 20:22). The word for spirit in the language of the Bible is the same as the word for "breath".

'Later, on the day of Pentecost, seven weeks after Jesus had first appeared to his disciples, they were all together in Jerusalem. The Bible records that, "Suddenly a sound like the blowing of a violent wind came from heaven and filled the whole house where they were sitting." They saw what looked like tongues of fire dancing on their heads and they were all filled with the Holy Spirit. This time the "breath of God" was not a gentle breeze, but a powerful wind which transformed the lives of the disciples. From a frightened bunch of men they changed to become bold and went out and changed the world.

'Just like breath transforms the bubbles we looked at earlier, into something beautiful and free, the breath of God transformed the disciples' lives. However, the Spirit of God is more than just the breath of God. The Bible tells us that he is a person, alongside God the Father and Jesus. "Breath" or "wind" gives us a picture of what he is like: felt but not seen, sometimes gentle, sometimes powerful, but always able to change peoples' lives in exciting ways. He is still doing that today in the lives of Christians in this town and all over the world.'

Pentecost - fire

Introduction

- **Aim:** To show that the transforming power of the fire of the Spirit is still at work all over the world.
- **Preparation:** Cooked and uncooked food, eg crisps and raw potato, or popcorn and raw corn; raw bacon, a pan, a camping gas-stove and matches.

Content

Get some volunteers out and feed them first the cooked and then the raw foods. Ask them what makes the difference ... Cooking, in other words heat; fire. It transforms what is inedible to most people into something we can eat and enjoy.

Light the stove and start cooking the bacon! Fire's power to transform is very useful to us, but those who have cooked while camping or over an open fire know how careful you have to be. Fire spreads very quickly.

Application and response

34

If not using this talk as a follow-up to the previous one, outline the background to the Pentecost story briefly. Read Acts 2:1–4. Continue with something along these lines:

'These people were "set on fire". From men who were fearful of the authorities they were transformed into fearless witnesses, telling on the streets of Jerusalem the amazing story of how Jesus came back from the dead. Just as fire quickly spreads, so these men's beliefs in Jesus and his resurrection spread like wildfire. Within a few years, with no radio or TV, no modern transport, that fire had spread throughout the Roman Empire.

'It continues to flare up today, but now it is affecting all the continents of the world. It flares up in Korea – and some of the biggest churches in the world are formed. It flares up in Africa – and thousands of people find they no longer need live in fear of the spirit world. It flares up in China – and the same miracles happen as we read about in the Bible.

'This fire heats a pan to transform a rasher of bacon into a tasty snack but the fire of the Holy Spirit can totally transform a person's life. That is as true today as it was on that first Pentecost when Peter said to the crowd, "Each one of you must turn away from his sins and be baptized in the name of Jesus Christ, so that your sins will be forgiven; and you will receive God's gift, the Holy Spirit"' (Acts 2:38).

For further information and help

British Youth for Christ and **Scripture Union** have local and regional schools staff who regularly take assemblies, lessons and support a large number of voluntary school Christian groups throughout the country. Both agencies are committed to working alongside churches and in many areas churches have worked together to appoint a BYFC or SU schools worker. Details of staff in your region who can advise, encourage and help resource school visitors are available on request from:

Scripture Union in Schools
130 City Road
London EClV 2NJ

British Youth For Christ
Cleobury Place
Cleobury Mortimer
Kidderminster
Worcs DY14 8JG

Christian Education in Nottingham Schools (CENS) publishes a termly broadsheet of assemblies for Junior and Secondary pupils called *Assembly Line*. Details from:

CENS
94 Burlington Road
Sherwood
Nottingham NG5 2GS